THE OFFICIAL
HECKLER
HANDBOOK

THE
OFFICIAL
HECKLER
HANDBOOK

The Ultimate Guide to Offending and Irritating the Enemy

Kevin Nelson

Illustrations by **Aaron Dana**

Guilford, Connecticut

An imprint of Rowman & Littlefield

Distributed by NATIONAL BOOK NETWORK

Copyright © 2016 by Kevin Nelson

British Library Cataloguing in Publication Information Available

Library of Congress Cataloging-in-Publication Data is available on file.

ISBN 978-1-4930-2451-3
ISBN 978-1-4930-2452-0 (e-book)

∞™ The paper used in this publication meets the minimum requirements of American National Standard for Information Sciences—Permanence of Paper for Printed Library Materials, ANSI/NISO Z39.48-1992.

CONTENTS

INTRODUCTION

Tiger Woods is striding down the fairway of the US Open with the earnest purposefulness that so distinguishes him on a golf course. But on this day he is not feeling very distinguished, for his game is a mess, like his reputation. Taunting reports in the media keep popping up like the gopher in *Caddyshack* about his spectacular, if unseemly, sex life. One of the juiciest tales involves a waitress at a pancake restaurant who partied with him at his love-shack mansion in Florida. It is a safe bet that the golfer he is walking with is not discussing any of these things with him and may not know about the rumors.

Somebody else does, though. This somebody else is a man who is watching Tiger play his Wednesday practice round. He is a heckler and he shouts, "Waffle House!"

The heckler's arrow strikes its target, because although Tiger does not stop walking, he looks back and points in the direction of the man who is standing along the edge of the fairway. His buddies join the fun. "Waffle House!" they all shout and laugh. "Waffle House!"

Jump to a recent NBA Finals game and LeBron James, who is to basketball what Tiger was to golf until Tiger's life on and off the course got scrambled. The charismatic Mr. All-Everything is walking off the floor after leading the Cleveland Cavaliers to a win. Fans and the media surround him court-side and snap pictures of him as he heads for the locker room, flanked by men in suits and uniforms whose job is to protect him in case something happens.

Suddenly something happens.

Heckling knows no gender boundaries.

A voice cries out, "LeBron, how does it feel to be a p*ssya**b*tch?" LeBron stops and turns and security responds too, all of them glaring back in the direction of the voice, which, shockingly, does not belong to a man. Disgust registers in James's face. The potty mouth belongs to a woman.

One of the men in suits comes forward and shouts, "Hey, watch your mouth, woman!" He repeats this warning as James moves on and the heckler—a pleasant-faced woman in her late 20s, in a yellow Golden State T-shirt, nicely made up, with her hair pulled back—meekly apologizes for her outburst. She seems genuinely contrite, the last person on earth you'd expect to be yelling profanities at a sporting event.

Heckling is a verbal pie in the face, and sometimes it can be an actual pie in the face. It also can be a whole bunch of people throwing pies at one another, like a slapstick bit in an old-time Mack Sennett comedy. Unexpectedly, too, it can be something else: a kind of dialog or conversation between the heckler and the heckled.

One more incident, this time from baseball. Tony Gwynn Jr., the son of the late Hall of Famer, is in right field for the Los Angeles Dodgers in a game against the Colorado Rockies at Coors Field. He is facing home plate, crouched in the outfielder's ready position as the pitcher delivers the ball and a heckler yells at Gwynn, "Hey, don't act like you're playing."

The pitch is called, and Gwynn stands up straight and moves his glove behind his back, actually his butt, and opens it. Then when the heckler in his nauseating Gilbert Gottfried voice starts yakking at him again, Gwynn is ready, opening and shutting his glove like he's manipulating the mouth of a ventriloquist's dummy.

"**Hey, don't act like you're playing.**"

Everybody around the heckler gets it and bursts into laughter.

The heckler keeps going, "Don't act like you don't hear me," but Gwynn surely hears him, because each time the man says something Gwynn's glove opens and shuts like it's the man's big mouth. It's a clever piece of improv comedy that only the right fielder and the fans behind him were aware of at the time, but now it has been seen by close to two million viewers on YouTube. After the inning ends Gwynn starts his walk back toward the Dodgers dugout, and there is some swagger to it. He knows he has bested a man whose goal was to torment him.

Heckling has long been a glorious/inglorious sports tradition. Choose the adjective that best describes your point of view. Many see heckling as a blight, a nuisance, profane, uncomfortable to be around, scary, possibly dangerous. Others find it entertaining and fun, like with the Tony Gwynn episode. There is a First Amendment right to free speech in America, and hecklers are part of that. Pro athletes make huge sums of money and they can stand to hear what fans think about them, even if—as LeBron's lady heckler showed—it's pretty raunchy stuff sometimes.

Besides, heckling can distract an opposing player and put him off his game, causing misery for his team and helping yours win. What is wrong with that?

However you line up in this debate—and you may see merits on both sides—none of these arguments actually speaks to the essential mysteries of heckling: that is, why do people do it and how do they do it best? Why did those guys shout "Waffle House!" at Tiger Woods when most people—most sane people, some would argue—would never dream of saying such an insulting thing to him?

This is only one of the many topics we will cover in *The Official Heckler Handbook*. This is a book for and about hecklers and for all the people who would never shout "Waffle House!" at Tiger Woods but who may be curious, and perhaps somewhat appalled as well, by those who do.

Curious and appalling. These are two more words to describe heckling, which so offends some people they feel it should be subject to strict limits, if not banned outright. Why do these people, including some of the most powerful figures in sports, dislike heckling? This seems as good a place as any to start. Let's peel away the onion and see what we find.

CHAPTER 1

- - - - - - - - - - - - - -

Why does everyone hate hecklers?
Or do they?

O n an episode of *Live with Kelly and Michael*, Michael Strahan, the ex-New York Giants defensive end who is cohost of the show, decided to ask the audience a question, a question virtually everyone can answer in the affirmative.

"How many of you have been to a sporting event?"

The studio audience responded with applause as Kelly Ripa, who was sipping from a mug of coffee, put down her mug and joined the clapping. She and Strahan sat at a table with their coffee, some papers, and a small American flag on it. With pert blond hair and in a fetching purple top, Ripa sat forward in her chair behind the table, smiling and nodding agreeably. But then Strahan asked a follow-up question, and her demeanor changed abruptly.

"But how many of you have ever heckled the athletes at a sporting event?"

"Oh, I would never heckle an athlete," Ripa said as she sat back in her chair and crossed her arms. Though still smiling her expression had become more thoughtful, more disapproving.

"Never. Why?" her cohost asked.

As an NFL veteran and Hall of Famer (and football TV analyst, in addition to his daytime talk show duties) who had heard heckling at every one of his away games and many of his home games too, Strahan remained upbeat. The idea of it did not seem to bother him nearly as much, and he went on to tell the story of a New York Knicks fan who had been heckling Carmelo Anthony so bad that he got tossed from Madison Square Garden and was now suing the team and the league for infringing on his free speech rights.

"Here's my whole thing," said Ripa, sitting forward again to explain how she felt. "It's one of those freedom of speech things, but it's a sporting event. There are kids there. Have some decorum, for heaven's sake. You know what I mean? There are kids there."

Her remarks met with enthusiastic applause from the audience members, who clearly shared her sentiments. Kids are off-limits, or should be. They should be spared the vulgar, disgusting, drunken vitriol that some fans spew at sporting events. Hecklers of this type send families heading for the exits and ruin a ballgame for anyone who has the misfortune to be sitting near them.

Dressed nattily in a brown blazer, crisp white shirt, and blue tie, Strahan, who has his own clothing line, was on board with all of this. What's more, he said, heckling doesn't even work. It did not upset him when he played; rather, it had the opposite effect. It motivated him.

"Trust me," he said. "I've been heckled. I've played in Philadelphia. But you know what they didn't realize—heckling was a motivation for a football player. Now there are some I wanted to jump up in the stands and pull the old Ron Artest on 'em. But I didn't do that."

This line, unlike the good-natured Philly remark, which drew laughs, fell flat, however, perhaps because there were not many hard-core sports fans in the audience and they did not get the reference. The reference was to one of the uglier episodes in recent NBA and sports history, when Artest, then playing for

Ron Artest before
he became Metta
World Peace.

the Indiana Pacers, and his teammate Stephen Jackson left the court and went up into the stands and became embroiled in a brawl with fans at a game against the Detroit Pistons at the Palace at Auburn Hills. The 2004 fight that came to be known as "the Malice at the Palace" occurred with less than a minute left in the fourth quarter. Pistons center Ben Wallace drove hard to the bucket and Artest fouled him even harder. Wallace pushed Artest angrily, as if wanting to trade blows with him. A referee jumped in to separate the two men, other players jumped in too, and the coaches rushed onto the court. Although there was a lot of pushing and shoving and threatening behavior,

Comic relief: What stand-ups say about hecklers

One non-sporting group who has terrible things to say about hecklers is stand-up comedians, who hate having their sets interrupted by shouted comments from "their enemies in the dark," as comic Jamie Kennedy puts it. "The No. 1 thing about hecklers," says Joe Rogan, "is 100 percent of them are douchebags." Fellow stand-up Rob Zombie describes the typical heckler as "some guy who lives in his parents' basement, who never had a girlfriend, telling Stephen Spielberg why he sucks."

Like athletes, comics often ply their trade in front of drunks, but unlike athletes, they get to verbally return fire. Keith Fields's standard retort when a heckler blurts something is: "I'm sorry, I don't speak **alcoholic**." Steve Hofstetter pretends he didn't hear the remark then says, "I don't know what you said but I'm sure it was stupid." Louie Anderson fantasizes about what he'd like to do to a heckler: "I always think it'd be fun to come on stage some night and shoot a heckler. 'Cause people would come back and see you and say, 'Don't [heckle] him. He killed a guy last week.'"

Stand-ups don't always hate their enemies in the dark, though. Sometimes hecklers say funny things, giving the performers on stage a chance to engage in witty repartee. Bryson Turner was doing a bit one night on having sex, saying, "This is how bad I was at sex the first time. The first time I ever had sex—"

"Yesterday?" said a woman in the audience interrupting him.

The room exploded in delight and Turner, smiling, acknowledging the cleverness of the jab, had to wait for the laughter to die down before he could respond.

"I'm glad you remember," he said to her.

The room erupted once more, and the comedian and the heckler, each having drawn comic blood, shook hands.

things were starting to calm down until a cup of beer came flying out of the stands and hit Artest in the head.

Calm no more. Enraged, Artest, who has since legally changed his name to Metta World Peace, bolted from the Pacers' bench and charged into the stands followed by his brother-in-arms, Jackson. The scene quickly devolved into an NBA public relations nightmare and a scary, scary encounter for all who were there, as both men threw punches at fans and landed them. Meanwhile the fans fought back, throwing beer and other things at the players while the melee spilled out of the stands and onto the court.

Eventually the Pacers left the floor, showered by more beer and objects, and peace was restored. But not without major repercussions from the NBA, which doled out suspensions to Artest, Jackson, and other players. It also beefed up security at its arenas and adopted a more stringent code of conduct for fans, warning them of eviction from games and arrest or prosecution for the worst offenses.

The fan who threw the inciting cup of beer did indeed get charged and do jail time, while the other fans who were involved received a beat-down of their own from the media. ESPN's John Saunders called them "a bunch of punks." His colleague Tim Legler, a former NBA guard, said that Artest and Jackson's reaction of going up into the stands was "somewhat justified" because of all the heckling they had gotten from fans during the game. "The racial slurs, throwing things, it's ridiculous," said Legler. "Often times at that point you just lose control emotionally."

He added, "You're going to hear people talking about how players have to show restraint. Most people—the average person on the street—they wouldn't show the kind of restraint that players do just listening to the heckling and abuse you take in the course of a game as a professional athlete."

The fans were out of control and they had it coming. That was the gist of it. They acted like thugs and they deserved rough justice. This was also what Kelly Ripa suggested should be done to that heckler in the Garden who had so harshed Melo's mellow.

"I think that after the game if there's a fan that's going cuckoo and cursing and screaming the entire game at, say, Carmelo Anthony," she said, "at the end of the game you hand him like a golden ticket and you say, 'You won a special prize.' Then you put him in a room and Carmelo walks in."

Here, the audience laughed and clapped, including Ripa's cohost, who added, "Yeah, close the door. See ya in five minutes."

Although Ripa went on to say that Anthony's presence alone would shock the heckler into deference and submission, no pummeling necessary, her point was clear and is shared by many in and out of the media. Hecklers are the jerkiest of jerks—they say—and worthy of our scorn and contempt, and here are only a few of the reasons why.

1. It's all about them.
The action on the field or the court matters less to the heckler than what he is doing and saying, and his self-absorption poisons the game for those who are not into the heckler the way the heckler is into himself. "Mostly," writes Ian Crouch of *The New Yorker*, "heckling is just one example of the pathetic fallacy of fandom, that those of us in the seats are part of the action, essential to our team's success—that we matter."

2. They say nasty things.

Painful examples of this abound. Here are two that were witnessed by Reddit contributors.

Baltimore Orioles catcher Greg Zaun is visiting Yankee Stadium, and Yankees fans welcome him to New York with lines such as:

"Hey Zaun, hope someone stabs you when you leave the park."

"Hope you get hit in the head."

"Hope your wife cheats on you."

"Hey Zaun, hope you get leukemia."

At another park, not in New York, in a prearranged spectacle a male fan gets down on one knee and proposes to his girlfriend in a live video feed on the stadium's big-screen

I now pronounce you heckled.

scoreboard. Close by are four drunks who taunt him and the girl at this most vulnerable of times.

"Don't do it!" they yell. "He's a no-good bum. You can do better than him. Who proposes at a ballgame? That rock is tiny. Find somebody with a job."

3. They mock even children.

Some hecklers do not just heckle *around* children, they heckle *at* them, such as the scurrilous individuals who were overhead insulting a batboy for doing a lousy job. A batboy!

4. They drink. And drink. And drink.

Cincinnati Reds second baseman Brandon Phillips had to listen to one obnoxious drunk heckle him all game long. Afterward Phillips sent a baseball over to him that carried this handwritten message: "Dear Drunk Guy, thank you 4 all the love and support. Now take this ball and shut the f**k up."

5. They are not funny.

People pay good money to see athletes play. They do not pay good money to see hecklers heckle, especially if a heckler's jokes land like—sorry for the heckler-like terminology—turds. Not entertaining your audience is death for hecklers and comedians alike.

6. They are idiots.

Bud Light once made a TV commercial in which it celebrated, in a mocking, Jon Stewart sort of way, what it called "Real Men of Genius." These geniuses were hecklers.

"Today we salute you, Mr. Pro Sports Heckler Guy," said the voiceover in the spot. "They say those who can't play, coach. Apparently those who can't coach sit 30 rows back shirtless, shouting obscenities."

Heckling in pop culture

Perhaps because people have such strong feelings about it, pro and con, heckling and hecklers appear frequently in pop culture. An annoying woman Kramer is dating heckles Jerry at a comedy club in a *Seinfeld* episode. The young Robert Downey Jr. does a riff on heckling in a screwball comedy he made with Rodney Dangerfield early in his career. The Heckle Depot, Bleacher Report, and Dr. Heckle are only three of the websites that revel in it. Twitter is awash with hecklers of every stripe, and YouTube shows comedy and sports heckler videos that draw millions of viewers.

Cartoons are another fertile area and have been for as long as there have been cartoons. In *The Heckling Hare*, from 1941, Bugs Bunny jumps onto the back of a dog he is torturing and asks, "Uh, let's see. What can I do to this guy? Hmm, I got it." Bugs's mischief leads the dog to plummet off a cliff, and when the rascally rabbit peers down to look at him lying on the ground far below, he says what lots of hecklers say after they've dissed a player from an opposing team: "Too bad. Ah, but the jerk had it coming to him."

Heckle and Jeckle were two wisecracking black birds that appeared in cartoons and comic books in the 1950s and '60s. Billed as "the talking magpies," they goofed on gullible dogs and many others, same as Bugs. Jeckle spoke like an upper-class Brit whereas Heckle was all Jersey or New York. Danny DeVito or Joe Pesci would be leading candidates to voice Heckle today.

On television in the late 1970s, Statler and Waldorf of *The Muppet Show* were two cranky old men—well, they were puppets—who heckled Rudolf Nureyev and other guest stars as well as other Muppets. After a sketch the camera would cut to Waldorf (the shorter, silver-haired one) and Statler (the taller, crankier one) commenting on it from their seats in a theater balcony.

"What was that?" asked Waldorf in one episode.

"It's called 'The Medium Sketch,'" answered Statler.

"The Medium Sketch?" echoed Waldorf.

"Yeah, it wasn't rare and it certainly wasn't well done," riffed Statler.

After Waldorf described one guest star as "a great little actress," Statler said, "Yes, and getting smaller all the time." Statler had a kindly mean streak like Don Rickles and could not resist trash-talking even his best friend. "Don't heckle me, you old fool," Waldorf told him once. "Heckle him!" Fortunately they both heckled all with equally good-spirited malice.

As the screen showed pictures of Barry Bonds, Alex Rodriguez, and other scandal-plagued ballplayers, the voiceover went on, "Thanks to you our team is armed with game-winning tips like 'Catch the ball,' 'Throw it,' 'You stink,' 'That sucks,' and 'What a bunch of losers.' So here's to you, O Sultan of Shouting. There may be no *I* in team, but thanks to you, there's always an *F* and a *U*."

7. They swear. A lot.

Yes they do, and this is one of the offenses that bring warnings from ushers and can get hecklers tossed.

8. They are racist pigs.

From George Stovey to Jimmy Claxton to Jackie Robinson, and from Robinson to Hank Aaron to Carl Crawford, the long history of baseball contains many instances of white fans hammering African Americans and other minorities simply for the color of their skin or their ethnic heritage. This has occurred in other sports too, and sadly, incidents of a racial nature still crop up from time to time in all sports.

9. They are sexist and homophobic pigs.

Some hecklers use the C-word (rhymes with "bunt") and the B-word (rhymes with "pitch"). They compare multimillion dollar athletes who jump from city to city and team to team to working girls on the street (rhymes with "score"). They gaily use anti-gay language such as the F-word (rhymes with "maggot"), and when Dallas Cowboys quarterback Tony Romo comes to town, they call him a disparaging term that rhymes with his last name, as if he plays like someone who wears a dress or some such nonsense.

10. They say stuff that makes no sense.

Hecklers ridicule a player's mother, father, family, wife, his multiple ex-wives, his multiple child support payments, whatever flaws they can find in his Wikipedia bio, his low batting average ("I bowl higher than you hit"), his poor free throw stroke ("Brick!" just as he lets go of the ball), where he went to college, the fact that he may not be able to spell "college," his size (fat, skinny, short, tall, whatever), his fishy name ("Hey Trout, I like Salmon!" a much cleverer line than it might seem, as Tim

If his last name is Trout, call him Salmon. And vice versa.

Salmon was a sweet-hitting Angel outfielder when Mike Trout was still in diapers), his looks, and especially for a major league ballplayer, his beard:

"Hey Blackmon, you look like a free-range buffalo!"

This comment, made by Los Angeles heckler and film-maker Bobby Crosby to bushy-faced Charlie Blackmon of the Colorado Rockies—and available for viewing, incidentally, on Crosby's YouTube channel—was followed up by more Crosby comments about the outfielder after he struck out looking and then was ejected for arguing the call. "Blackmon," he shouted, "you're out, you omnivore. Free-range buffalo kicked out of game."

Crosby's nonsensical shtick drew laughs, unlike a lot of hecklers who make stuff up, say completely random things, and say whatever is on their mind, even if it's nothing.

11. They are unoriginal.

Question: How many times can hecklers shout "You suck!" at players and expect the people sitting around them to smile and laugh hysterically?

Answer: Apparently it is limitless, as we discover in chapter 8, "The incredible, inevitable, unavoidable 'You suck!' chapter." It is a chapter you should look forward to because it is enter-taining and does not suck.

12. They have small penises.

Okay, this one is a little bit . . . out there. No one really believes hecklers have small penises, except possibly for The Fum-ble's sports babe personality Crystal Marie Denha, who once opened her online show by saying, "There's not much more I hate than hecklers, especially sporting event hecklers. They're loud, they're annoying, and they probably have a penis no longer than my pinkie." Besides, women are known to heckle too.

13. They interfere with players doing their jobs.
This is a common complaint, as noted by online basketball reporter Elie Seckbach in a piece about heckling in the NBA: "Now imagine getting heckled every time you go to work. Well, that's what happens to NBA players." Seckbach asked some players about the worst things that fans had said to them. Five-foot-five Denver Nuggets guard Earl Boykins, the Gary Coleman of pro basketball, said, "One of the fans yelled, 'I thought this was an NBA game. I didn't know this was a high school game.'"

14. They are, collectively speaking, a thumb in the eye of authority.
"Heckling can be seen as a disruption or a challenge to power," psychologist Pamela Rutledge told a reporter in an interview on heckling, and let's be real here: Powerful people typically do not like that. These include athletes, coaches, managers, referees and umpires, front office executives, owners, luxury box grandees, league commissioners, arena and stadium officials, corporate sponsors, TV and radio networks, and media personnel who have a vested interest in the lucrative world of pro sports.

15. When all is said and done, hecklers are just bags of hot air.

For all the disruptions they cause, hecklers ultimately make no difference in whether teams win or lose or how players play. They are nonfactors. As Michael Strahan alluded to in his remarks on *Live with Kelly and Michael*, they may even hurt the team they're rooting for and motivate the opposition to try harder.

But hold on, wait a minute. The segment on heckling did not end there, with Ripa suggesting how Carmelo Anthony's tormentor ought to be locked in a room with him and Strahan explaining how hecklers made him play better when he was on the Giants. Rather, he finished up by telling his favorite taunt ever directed at him. Naturally it came from fans of the New York Jets, the Giants' intracity rival, and it occurred at a game at the Meadowlands.

Jets fans chanted, "Ortho-dontist! Ortho-dontist!"

As he told this story and delivered the punch line, Strahan flashed his bright, Letterman-like gap-toothed grin, and Ripa and the studio audience enjoyed laughing along with the joke, a joke that suddenly sent the entire discussion up to that point careening in a new direction like an automobile thrown into reverse. The hecklers were making fun of the gap in his teeth, but why was everyone so cheery about it, the object of the taunts included?

You mean to say there might be something more to this heckling business than just dumb crude punks saying dumb crude sh*t? You mean there might even be socially redeeming aspects to it, that it might even be . . . fun? Not only fun and entertaining but useful, valuable, worthwhile? More investigation is clearly required.

To football Hall of Famer Michael
Strahan—"Ortho-dontist!"

CHAPTER 2

Hunter Pence eats pizza with a fork

On the first day of August in 2014, one of the most unique and uplifting moments in heckling history occurred at Citi Field in New York in a Friday night game between the hometown Mets and the visiting San Francisco Giants.

Though no one thought it was unique at the time. In fact, nobody paid much attention to it at all until the fifth inning, when a TV camera turned to the seats and showed two teenage boys standing side by side, each holding a sign above his head.

One boy had blond hair and was wearing a No. 4 Mets jersey. His bright yellow sign read HUNTER PENCE PUTS KETCHUP ON HIS HOT DOGS.

The other boy had dark hair and a No. 21 Mets jersey. His neon green sign said HUNTER PENCE EATS PIZZA WITH A FORK.

For all the trendsetting buzz these two boys—who were never identified in the blaze of tweets and posts that followed shortly—would set into motion, their signs elicited a puzzled, ho-hum reaction from broadcaster Mike Krukow, the ex-major leaguer who was working the telecast that night for the Giants.

"They know he likes kale," Krukow said on the air, mulling over the boys' messages and trying to figure out what they meant because they were clearly not the usual heckler fare seen at major league parks. "He's a healthy eater."

The shot on screen cut from the boys and their signs to Pence in right field. (Pence said later he never saw the signs that night, and why would he? The boys were two tiny figures in a loud and restless sea of people, and he had a game to play, after all.) Besides his All-Star prowess in the field and at bat,

Does accusing a player of eating pizza this way throw him off his game?

the curly-haired, scraggly-bearded right fielder is known for being a fitness buff who adheres to the paleo diet—no carbs, no processed or refined foods, heavy on the meat and veggies—and the deeply intense, almost trance-like expression that comes over his face during high-pressure moments in a game. It is not conscious or a deliberate act on his part; it is just what he does, how he responds to pressure. Pence calls it his "weird cave man" face.

But the boys weren't riffing on that; they were making obscure references to something else, whatever it was, and it befuddled more observers than just Krukow. The *New York Daily News* called the signs "strange." They were not talking smack, they were talking . . . huh? Pizza with a fork? Ketchup on his dogs? What gives?

Many people watching on TV—and following on social media, after a GIF of the TV clip (the boys and their signs, followed by Pence) appeared endlessly on Vine and elsewhere—did get it, though. And even if some did not quite get it, they dug the whole vibe of what the boys were up to, especially when they showed up again on Saturday with more signs trolling the Giants star:

HUNTER PENCE BRINGS 13 ITEMS TO THE EXPRESS LANE

HUNTER PENCE CAN'T SHUFFLE PLAYING CARDS

HUNTER PENCE THINKS GAME OF THRONES IS JUST OK

"They're back!" announced MLB on its Twitter feed that day. "The @hunterpence trolling continues at Citi Field."

Friday night there were just the two, Saturday there were more, and by Sunday afternoon, the third game of a four-game

Sign language

A sign is a silent form of heckling, such as the one a hockey fan held up above a referee who was standing on the ice, resting for a moment against the boards. The sign had an arrow on it pointing down to the ref's head. Inside a thought bubble it said, "I'm the biggest IDIOT ever!!!!"

The classic hockey thought-bubble sign.

A sign is a kind of predigital-era throwback. Unless you get lucky and your sign gets shown on TV like the Hunter Pence boys—or the college football fans whose signs make it onto ESPN's *Game Day* program—the only people who will ever see it are those sitting near you in the park.

A sign does not typically contain a photo or an image, like a meme. It is a few words or a phrase at most, hand-lettered or scrawled with crayons or marking pens onto a poster or cardboard. Most signs are not professionally done and look nothing like the commercial electronic signs you see everywhere in modern stadiums. They are crafted on the kitchen table at home or in the dorm room or improvised in the parking lot at a tailgate party. And they are not obscene, because obscene signs quickly get confiscated.

Nonetheless, a sign can still deliver a message with a sharp point. After it was revealed that Los Angeles Clippers owner Donald Sterling had made derogatory remarks about African Americans, saying that his girlfriend should not bring any of her black friends to Clippers games—remarks that triggered a national controversy about race and cost him control of the team and a lifetime ban by the NBA—two Golden State basketball fans made their own statement about the issue at a game in Oakland.

One was black, the other white. Both in their thirties, both in Warriors jerseys, both friends. The black guy held a sign above his head with an arrow pointing down to him. It said, I'M BLACK.

The other guy, the white guy, stood next to him. His sign had an arrow pointing to his friend and it read, I BROUGHT A BLACK GUY 2 THE GAME. Somehow the two of them standing together, holding the signs, their smiling faces a reflection of their common humanity, made their message all the stronger.

set, lots and lots of fans had caught up with all the fun that was being had at the expense of Hunter Pence in Mets land.

HUNTER PENCE CAN'T PARALLEL PARK

HUNTER PENCE LIKES THE GODFATHER 3

HUNTER PENCE WHISPERS SORRY WHEN HE CATCHES A FLY BALL

HUNTER PENCE EATS SUB SANDWICHES SIDEWAYS

These and other signs—Hunter Pence prefers baths and Hunter Pence hates bacon, for example—sprouted across the park like crocuses in the spring, all handwritten, all thought up, laughed over (possibly fueled by an adult beverage or two), and then giddily held up by New York baseball fans not normally known for their subtlety but who, in the spirit of the thing, adopted the boys' gently chiding tone. Less gentle were the Bronx cheers dumped on the outfielder on Twitter.

"How does it feel to be so terribly owned, Hunter Pence?" read one tweet. "Mets fans drop some sick burns on Hunter Pence," said another. "Are you going to defend yourself Hunter Pence," chipped in a Deadspin blogger, "or let this dude trash talk your parallel parking skills?"

The Giants won three of four games in the series and beat the Mets 9–0 on Sunday. Pence went 3-for-5, hit two home runs and a double, and knocked in four runs and scored three, so all the sick burns did not exactly throw him into a slump. After the game the media asked him about the signs and he said he'd never even seen *Godfather 3*. "I don't think I've ever seen that one," he said. "I know what *The Godfather* is, but I don't think I've ever watched any of the movies in their entirety."

After New York the Giants left for a Tuesday night game in Miller Park in Milwaukee, where more signs bloomed—these from Brewers fans who saw what was going on in New York and wanted a piece of the action:

HUNTER PENCE STILL HAS A BLOCKBUSTER CARD

HUNTER PENCE LIVES IN A VAN DOWN BY THE RIVER

HUNTER PENCE WISHES HE WAS A LITTLE BIT TALLER

HUNTER PENCE HAS SHARKNADO INSURANCE

Every sign was white with a Kohl's logo in the upper right-hand corner. Kohl's, whose corporate headquarters are in Milwaukee, saw a positive way to promote itself and distributed blank placards at the park for fans, who then wrote their messages and displayed them from their seats or paraded around the aisles with them.

What happened next was yet another twist in the story. Hecklers heckle for many reasons but all who do it, whatever their motive, are seeking to connect, somehow, some way, with the object of their derision. This was true for the boys too, and in this, as in so many other ways, they succeeded wonderfully. Hunter Pence responded.

Hecklers are seeking to connect with the object of their derision.

One thing to remember about heckling is that professional athletes do it all the time to one another. They spit seeds at their teammates being interviewed on TV, stand behind them on camera and make faces, toss buckets of water on them, and smash them with cream pies. They bust each other's balls in the dugout, locker room, bus, airplane, and hotel bar. But the guys doing the ball-busting are fellow players, not the unwashed sports proletariat, and this makes all the difference in the world.

Another thing to keep in mind is that especially in base-ball—which has a centuries-old tradition of heckling, whose structure and setting are particularly conducive to it, and which attracts the most hecklers of any sport—it provides entertainment not just for fans but for the players as well. A baseball game can last three or more hours, unfolding at a pace that would make a snail feel comfortable, the sun blazing down on a drowsy midweek afternoon in summer. The spec-tators, like the men on the field, may feel drowsy themselves or hungover. Played on a field with large swaths of open real estate, the action can be sparse and intermittent. There are long stretches of repetition and boredom that make even the most devoted fan lose interest at times.

Enter the heckler or a boisterous, unruly, sh*t-disturbing gang of them. San Francisco's cross-bay American League rival is Oakland, and whenever Pence plays there the Athletics fans crowding into the seats around his station in right never give him the silent treatment like the sign-bearers in New York. "Honestly, I just get emotional out there," he said, describing what it's like to be heckled at the Coliseum. "The fans out there—they've got the drums. In my sleep I'm hearing [the drums banging] and 'Pence, you suck!' It's like it gets embedded in your brain and so for me it's like 'Nah, dude,' I'm going to show you I don't suck."

In one game against the A's, Pence attempted a sliding catch on a sinking line drive and missed, and the ball skipped past him for extra bases for the batter. Cue the "You suck!" chants and barnyard noises from the Oakland drummers. Later in the same game the speedy outfielder made up for this lapse with a dazzling catch of a fly ball that shut down an Athletics rally and shut the fans up. Tormenting his tormentors, he

Does Hunter Pence whisper "Sorry" when he catches a fly ball?

cupped his right hand over his ear as if to say, "I can't hearrrr-rrrr you." Pound that, fellas.

This is what happens all the time, in small ways and large, between hometown fans and hecklers and the visiting players they are rooting against, in ballparks all across the land: a sporting game of give and take enjoyed, at times, by both sides. Here are only two such incidents.

1. At PNC Park in Pittsburgh, the Atlanta Braves are in town for a night game against the Pirates. In left field for the Braves is Matt Diaz, who, as outfielders are wont to do, takes steps around the grass between pitches, repositioning himself or just moving to move, because he has energy and has to express it. But here, a voice follows his every move. When Diaz steps left a heckler in the left field bleachers yells, "Left!" Then when he steps right the same guy yells, "Right!" And so on: "Left . . . right . . . left . . . right," continuously as Diaz moves around between pitches.

This is a tried-and-true heckling technique, variations of which have been done since the days of Ruth and Cobb. One is to echo the fielder's left-right steps until he comes to a stop, at which time you yell, "Stationary!" When he starts moving again you start in with your deal again. The point is to get the player thinking about something other than what he is supposed to, and it can irritate the hell out of some guys—although not Matt Diaz on this night. Tonight he is messing with the heckler rather than the other way around, dragging one leg behind him, hopping on one foot, lifting a leg high off the ground, and picking his feet up in short pitter-patter steps. His unpredictable movements throw the heckler off his left-right-left-right cadence, forcing him to speed up or slow down—on Diaz's

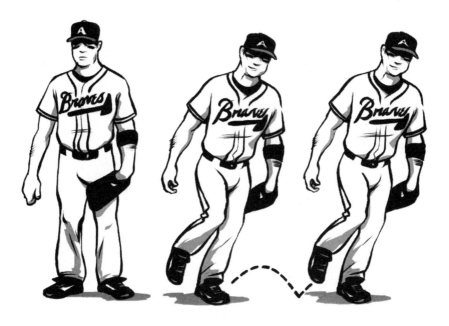

Matt Diaz bested the old dance-step heckle.

whim, not his. The heckler knows he has been owned and says, "You got me, Diaz," and laughs.

2. More Diaz, or in this case, Die-az. Now the good-natured Braves outfielder is in New York for a day game with the Mets at Citi Field, which is so devoid of paying customers that virtually everyone in the park can hear this one guy in the bleachers: "Hey Die-az. I know you hear me. Nobody likes you. Hey Die-az, go back to Little League and learn how to hit."

The heckler, with a voice like he could be a bouncer for the Bada Bing Club, pronounces it "Die-az" probably on purpose and perhaps to emphasize the "Die" part of it. "Hey Die-az," he says, now clowning on him for his footwear, "your shoes are untied. Check your laces, you bum. You got two different-colored socks on, Die-az."

Without turning to face the heckler, Diaz lifts first his right leg, then his left, showing off his socks for each. They are a matched set, contrary to the guy's claims, and the fans in the seats all around the heckler laugh and applaud this witty rejoinder, recognizing, as Ian Crouch says, that "the ballplayer had heard, and in a modern version of an old tradition, he'd looked back and tipped his cap." So it was with Hunter Pence when he responded to the Hunter Pence sign-makers, although this being the digital age, the man who allegedly puts ketchup on his hot dogs and eats pizza with a fork tipped his cap on Instagram and Twitter.

On Thursday, with the Giants in Milwaukee and the sign craze blowing up on social media and everywhere else, Pence did the equivalent of a Matt Diaz two-step or a Tony Gwynn Jr. glove flap and posted a meme on Instagram with a photograph of himself in a library reading a book. It said, "Hunter Pence returns library books before they're due so others can enjoy them as well."

Pence had gotten in the game too and was poking fun at himself. Another of his memes showed him and his girlfriend with the tagline "Hunter Pence makes his girlfriend watch the Weather Channel for fun."

And in a nonrebuttal rebuttal to one of the popular favorites, another one featured a photo of him wearing a big grin and sitting in a gleaming white Mercedes convertible in a car showroom. It said, "Hunter Pence can't parallel park."

In an interview a few days later with Chris Rose and Kevin Millar on the MLB Network, Pence explained that all of this got started the day before the two teenagers put up the signs at

Citi Field, when the Giants arrived in town and had an off day in New York with nothing to do and time to burn. "We're in New York, we have an off day, and we go to a diner," recalled Pence. "Me being the huge *Seinfeld* fan I am, I'm like, if I'm

Social media for hecklers

The Hunter Pence sign phenomenon could not have happened without social media, at least not in the way it did. Social media is changing the world, and it has changed heckling too. Hecklers need to get with it, if they are not already, and here are a few of the basics.

Smart phone: Obvious, right? Heckling with a phone without online access is like opening a bottle of wine without a corkscrew. You can still do it, but it is much easier with the right tool. The right tool for hecklers is a smart phone; it lets you Google players and look up their Wikipedia bios at the game, on the spot. You can also shoot video of what you're doing and upload it to YouTube.

Twitter: The best social network for hecklers is Twitter, which perplexes many novice users at first. Give it a chance: It will grow on you, and its 140-character limit on tweets is just right for dissing and being dissed. Sure, you will make mistakes at first, but so what? You will figure it out soon enough and find it to be a newsy, entertaining way to connect with like-minded practitioners of the art of the heckle.

Instagram: Instagram is another connectivity creator. Tons of athletes and celebrities have Instagram and Twitter accounts where they post pictures and information about themselves. Follow them and you can see all the cool parties they're going to that you're not. You might post something that catches an athlete's attention, and he may decide to share it or retweet it on his feed. It happens. Then again, he may tell you to bugger off, which also happens.

Memes: Memes are like online signs or posters. They are easy to do; how-to advice is but a click away. They are so easy to do that whenever a major brouhaha erupts in sports, memes pop up instantly everywhere, mocking the figures involved. This was true with Deflategate, when the NFL accused Tom Brady and the New England Patriots of underinflating footballs. One meme showed Brady holding a sign that said, "To me, those balls are perfect." Another was a close-up of him hugging his coach Bill Belichick. "You know what I like, Coach?" said Brady, whispering in his ear. "Soft balls." Similar was the one with the bare-chested quarterback looking too sexy for his shirt and fondling a football: "I like my balls . . . soft."

Last word: On a personal note, this author feels strongly that the best heckling is done live, in person, at the game. Hecklers who go out to the park are showing their faces to the world, and there is a virtue in that.

in a New York diner, I'm gonna take a picture of me drinking coffee—you know, with that line I love from *Seinfeld*: 'These pretzels are making me thirsty.'"

So he threw the post up on Instagram and "New Yorkers took off with it." Two of those New Yorkers were the two boys, true-blue *Seinfeld* fans as well, because the lines about how New Yorkers should never put ketchup on their hot dogs or eat pizza with anything but their hands originally came from the show. The boys had the cleverness to turn them on Pence, who "loved it. I loved the comedy." One meme he especially liked showed him in his weird caveman face with the words "Hunter Pence eats kale so you don't have to."

It is a good thing Pence enjoyed it all, because it followed him the rest of the season, wherever he played, with fans parading signs around the park and cutting up on Instagram and Twitter (#HunterPenceSigns). They ragged on him for his taste in music—

HUNTER PENCE LISTENS TO NICKELBACK

His driving—

HUNTER PENCE STOPS AT YELLOW LIGHTS

HUNTER PENCE DRIVES A PRIUS

His personal habits—

HUNTER PENCE USES BENDY STRAWS

HUNTER PENCE WEARS SOCKS WITH SANDALS

HUNTER PENCE STAYS UP LATE TO CALL JAKE FROM STATE FARM

His lack of caring for animals—

HUNTER PENCE WILL DO ABSOLUTELY NOTHING FOR A KLONDIKE BAR

And they really got on him for his use of technology—

HUNTER PENCE STILL USES MYSPACE

HUNTER PENCE HAS AN AOL EMAIL ADDRESS

HUNTER PENCE BOUGHT A MAC AND INSTALLED WINDOWS

HUNTER PENCE USES INTERNET EXPLORER

HUNTER PENCE REPLIES BY SENDING "K"

HUNTER PENCE OWNS A FLIP PHONE

HUNTER PENCE ALWAYS SAFELY EJECTS HIS FLASH DRIVE

The Giants finished second in the National League West that season, qualifying for the playoffs as a wild card team. They beat Pittsburgh (wild card playoff), Washington (NL division series), and St. Louis (league championship series) in succession, encountering Hunter Pence heckling at every stop. In the World Series they traveled to Kansas City to meet the upstart Royals, whose fans signed off on the matter as well:

HUNTER PENCE TAGS UP ON GROUND BALLS

HUNTER PENCE LIKES MONDAY MORNINGS

HUNTER PENCE THINKS HE'S IN KANSAS

One Royals fan went so far as to put up a row of signs along the front lawn of his house:

HUNTER PENCE CONDITIONS BEFORE HE SHAMPOOS

HUNTER PENCE WATCHES THE WNBA

HUNTER PENCE LIKES FISH STICKS

And the cruelest cut of all, at least from the perspective of Kansas City, where the beef and steaks are to die for, he installed this sign:

HUNTER PENCE HATES BBQ

Unfortunately for the Royals, they didn't have quite enough to beat Pence and the Giants, who won a gripping seven-game series and took home their third world championship trophy in five years, a remarkable run. Remarkable for the Giants, yes, but not for this heartbroken fan, who ripped the signs from his lawn after the final out and tossed them in the trash.

CHAPTER 3

"Darrr-ryl . . . Darrr-ryl . . . Darrr-ryl . . ."

In his MLB interview with Hunter Pence, ex-major leaguer turned broadcaster Kevin Millar said how much he enjoyed the gently chiding nature of the pizza-with-a-fork and owns-a-flip-phone signs and wondered why more heckling can't be like that. "It's nice friendly banter that I like," said Millar, who played for a handful of teams in his decade-plus in the bigs. "There's no, like, angry [taunts]. We know 'You suck,' we've heard all those. But it's nice friendly banter. I like that."

Hecklers hear such criticism all the time, in and out of sports. Why do they have to be so mean? Why can't they be nicer?

The answer lies in the word itself. *Heckler*, Jamie Kennedy's movie about what stand-up comedians think of hecklers and how they deal with them, begins with this definition: "Heckler [noun]—one who tries to embarrass, harass, and/or annoy someone speaking or performing in public with gibes, questions, and objections." Note the verbs: embarrass, harass, annoy. And the nouns: gibes, questions, objections. One could easily add another verb, interrupt, to the list. Hecklers do that plenty too.

If we go back to the ancient origins of the word, we learn still more. "Heckle" is originally an English term that dates back hundreds of years, although a family working the land in West Sussex or Yorkshire in the early 1800s would have had a much different understanding of it than we do today. A heckle as they knew it was a tool for working with hemp and flax. The heckle tool, also known as a "hatchel," was a hard wooden brush with pointed metal spikes or teeth. To modern eyes it looks like a

Ye olde heckle or
hatchel is used
for—torture?!?

crude handheld instrument of torture, but it was made tough because it had a tough job to do: splitting and beating down raw flax and hemp fibers in order to convert them to other uses. Many people today associate hemp with cannabis, from which marijuana comes, but it has many more applications than that, such as clothing, textiles, rope, paper, and as a building material. People on the farm broke those useful but knotty fibers down by hand, with heckle tools.

In the Oxford English Dictionary, 1901 edition, the first two definitions of "heckle" have to do with the tool and combing out the hemp and flax, which is a key ingredient in linens. Not until the third definition do we come to a more contemporary sense of the word: "to catechize severely, with a view to discover the weak points of the person interrogated."

Over the centuries the heckle tool has mostly faded into the agrarian past, but Aaron Dana's modern illustration may be useful to keep in mind as we delve further into all the terrible, horrible, no-good things that hecklers say. A heckle, in its raw form, is a tool with sharp, nail-like 6-inch spikes. Those spikes can cut your finger or hand if you're not careful. The job of those spikes is to split, scrape, straighten, comb, beat down, rip, pull apart, and cut.

Nothing nice about it some days.

Hecklers attack weakness, and the first place they usually find it is in a player's name. What may be a source of strength or family pride to the player is merely an opportunity to take out ye olde heckle tool and go to scraping. Hecklers deliberately mispronounced outfielder Marquis Grissom's first name, calling him "Mar-kwiss." Third baseman Evan Longoria gets serenaded

Where to heckle at a baseball game: The bleachers

This is the classic venue for baseball hecklers. The bleachers are the uncovered seats or benches in the outfield sections of left, center, or right field. Sit in one of these areas and you can proudly claim the title of "Bleacher Bum" and launch verbal grenades at the outfielder nearest to where you are sitting.

If the player happens to have his back to you and your view is only of his firm manly buttocks, no matter. *He can still hear you.* So it was when the Yankees came to Shea to play the Mets in a Subway Series, and one Mets heckler was picking on Yankee center fielder Johnny Damon, trashing him for his looks, long hair, rotten throwing arm, and yes, his butt. Finally Damon turned around and wiggled his sweet cheeks for the crowd, and all in the bleachers roared their approval.

with chants of "Eva, Eva," feminizing his first name. Last names tend to offer more possibilities. "Hey Werth," goes a predictable line often directed at slugger Jason Werth, "you're worthless." (Werth also draws jeers for his long-haired, wooly-bearded Appalachian backwoods look. "Hey Duck Dynasty," they yell.) What hecklers say to catcher Brian McCann is clever: "Brian McCann? More like Brian McCan't!"

When reliever Marc Rzepczynski got the call from the San Diego Padres bullpen in the late innings of a game, one guy shouted, "I'd like to buy a vowel, Marc." Ever hear the song "Camptown Races?" The lyrics go, "Camptown ladies sing a song, doo-dah, doo-dah," etc. If you'd like, you can join other hecklers and sing this song to first baseman Lucas Duda when he appears at your park. Even coaches are not immune. Glenn Sherlock hears "Where's Watson?" everywhere he goes.

(See, Watson was Sherlock Holmes's sidekick and Glenn's last name is . . . aw, fuhgeddaboudit. A heckle, like a joke, is pretty much DOA if you have to explain it. Better to just shake your head and move on to the next one.)

Insulting a guy's name is one thing, but if you can insult a guy's name *and* throw in a lewd sexual reference, that's the hecklers' Daily Double. Anyone named Dick is fair game. Catcher Matt Wieters hears such timeless witticisms as "Wieters got no wiener!" Pitchers Charlie Furbush, Doug Fister, and Madison Bumgarner all have names with sexual connotations, opening the floodgates for those with minds of a certain bent. And who calls minor leaguer Brian Bocock by his proper name? It must always be "Boo-cock," just as major leaguer Jay Bruce is "Brucebag," like douchebag.

Some gags are not funny and never will be. They should be shot and left for dead and never spoken of again. But there's another class of jokes that are stupid or annoying at first but get funnier with repetition. For example, the hilarious gag in *The Family Guy* when Stewie tries to get the attention of his mother, who is resting on her bed. "Mom, Mom, Mom, Mommy, Mommy, Mama, Mama, Ma, Ma, Mum, Mummy . . ." he says to her, rattling on and on and on until finally she cracks and asks him what he wants. "Hi," he chirps, and runs from the room ecstatic that his little prank has succeeded.

Outfielder Torii Hunter must have felt like Stewie's mom the night a heckler in the bleachers kept yelling "Torrr-iiiii," pausing for a beat and then adding, "With two *i*'s." Inning after inning he would repeat this sequence—"Torrr-iiiii," beat, "with two *i*'s"—until the sheer goofy redundancy of it started drawing laughter, including from Hunter himself.

It is a well-known fact that Chipper Jones of the Atlanta Braves was one of the game's best third basemen for many years. Less well known is his actual first name, which prompted one Miami heckler to bellow it out every time he moved into

Where to heckle at a baseball game: The bullpen

The location of the bullpen depends on the park. Some parks put their bullpens in special areas beyond the outfield fence. Others place them on the field along the right and left field foul lines. Many bullpens provide an ideal vantage point for heckling at a major league ballpark, for you can sometimes stand above the visiting team's relievers, catchers, and bullpen coaches and yell stuff at them.

Do your thing before a game or during. You're close enough to be heard clearly and thus can make a real nuisance of yourself, reminding the catchers and pitchers that they are, after all, backups—and may even be backups to the backups. "The only difference between you and us," one heckler shouted to bullpen catcher Todd Greene at a game, "is you have better seats for the game, loser. Take your shin guards off. You're never getting in the game."

Bullpen hecklers.

Do not be disturbed if the players ignore you, or try to; the last word always belongs to the one with the quickest wit. There was the fan who asked a pitcher who was warming up, "Hey, can I get a ball?" When the pitcher blew him off, the fan replied, not missing a beat, "That's okay, I'll get one when you pitch."

the on-deck circle and batter's box: "Laaaarrry! Laaaarrry!" Other fans gradually started to listen for it and join in, although Larry himself probably wasn't too thrilled. A similar thing once occurred at Safeco Field in Seattle. Each time a visiting Yankee would come to the plate, a fan in the seats would loudly announce his name, then follow it with "You're washed up!" "At first," said a Reddit contributor who was there, "it was kinda stupid, but after the second time through the order, I couldn't help but laugh every time." (This is good heckling technique. Here's another thing to say after repeating a player's name: "Yer a bum!")

Ryan Braun gets heckled for his admitted steroid use—fans have waved syringes at him—and his nickname: He is known as "the Hebrew Hammer" for his Jewish faith, though less evolved types prefer "the Herpes Hammer." But at a night game at PNC Park in Pittsburgh one heckler stretched his last name out so far it became a punch line all by itself: "Braunnnnnn . . . you blew it. Let's see some hustle. Hey Braunnnnnn, you got another K on your record. Strike out against the Pirates—that's weak."

After persuading a few of his friends to join him in a group sing-along of "Braunnnnnn . . ." the heckler, whose voice sounded like old car brakes squeaking, continued to pour it on the left fielder: "Hey Braun, you better stop playing with your junk out there. You should have taken care of that in the hotel. Hey you Braun, you wear a jock strap or some boxer briefs? I bet you ain't wearing any drawers under there. And you're probably getting a hard-on from me. After that strikeout you need something to bring you up. Hey Braunnnnnn . . ."

Of course, to Pirates fans, this crude bit of doggerel is a nothing burger compared to one of the all-time great

Where to heckle at a baseball game: Visitors' dugout

Another good place to heckle is behind or around the visiting team's dugout, particularly when the out-of-towners are taking batting practice. Get as close as you can to the batting cage and make comments when they're taking their swings.

After the game begins, a seat in this general area affords you close proximity to their dugout, on-deck circle, batter's box, pitcher's mound, infielders, and first-base coach (if the visitors' dugout is on this side). First-base coach? Sure, why not heckle him too? First-base coaches are typically middle-aged or older retired ballplayers. They fidget constantly, and one amusing thing to do with a group is to say "Beep!" like the Road Runner every time the coach takes a step. Beep, beep, beeping some guys can drive them nuts.

One group of hecklers we heard of spent an entire game heckling a first-base coach, him and him only. "You're a first-base coach," they shouted ceaselessly, "a first-base coach. Get real!" The fans sitting nearby found this behavior rather odd at first, but after a while got into the sheer absurdist nature of the commentary. A first-base coach indeed. Get real!

name-based heckle chants in recent baseball history: "Cue-to . . . Cue-to . . . Cue-to . . ."

The chanting took place at PNC Field, and those who were there that night or who watched it on TV need hardly be reminded of the circumstances of the moment—the 2013 National League Wild Card Game between the hometown Pirates and the rival Cincinnati Reds. One game, loser goes home. Starting for the visitors was Johnny Cueto (pronounced Qway-toe), the Dominican Republic–born right-hander who made it through the first inning unscathed but ran into major trouble in the second, created in part by the 40,000-plus Pirates fans sarcastically singing his name in unison:

"Cue-to . . . Cue-to . . . Cue-to . . ."

Pittsburgh started the inning with a home run by Marlin Byrd, followed by an out. Up stepped the powerful Russell Martin, and the chants grew stronger and stronger like peals of thunder from an approaching storm. On the mound the long-haired Cueto rubbed up the ball, clearly unnerved by having all that vocal energy pouring down on him. So unnerved was he that the ball slipped from his glove and dribbled a few feet away onto the grass. As he quickly went to grab it, the fans went wild and the chanting grew more thunderous still, if that was possible.

Ernie Johnson, who was doing the play-by-play for TBS that night, said, "This standing-room-only crowd is trying to get under Johnny Cueto's skin, and they just might be."

There was no "might" about it, for on his very next pitch—the one after the ball dropped—Cueto delivered a belt-high fastball that Martin deposited deep into the left field bleachers, beginning a new round of chants and sending the Pirates to a 6-2 win and the next round of the playoffs.

Sharing the broadcast booth with Johnson was Ron Darling, a former New York Mets pitcher who confirmed how completely Cueto had lost his grip: "I know playing on the road can rattle you sometimes, but this is ridiculous." Lending a historical perspective to the evening, Darling said, "I haven't heard a chant like this since 'Darryl' at Fenway Park in the 1980s."

He should know because he was there, a Mets teammate of Darryl Strawberry, who endured a Fenway Park heckling by Boston Red Sox fans that may have been even more humiliating than Cueto's. This was 1986, Game 5 of the World Series, Mets v. Red Sox, series tied at two games apiece. The score was 4-1 Sox in the eighth, but the Mets had just plated a run with the dangerous Strawberry (27 home runs on the season) up at bat with a man on base. But he fouled out anemically to kill the rally and end the inning, and when the right fielder

Where to heckle at a baseball game: Behind home plate

Here, only a protective screen separates you from the heart of the action: pitcher, batter, catcher, umpire. Fans on both sides heckle the last group and have done so since Alexander Cartwright first suited up for the Knickerbockers. Shouting "Flip over the plate and read the damn directions!" when the ump makes a bad call is an old-school heckling line, but it may still have some life left in it and it's yours free of charge if you care to use it. "Get off your knees, ump, you're blowing the game," while also old school, is the kind of profane chatter that can get you warned or tossed if you're not careful.

"Hey, ump! Flip over the plate and read the damn instructions!"

Better, perhaps, to leave the ump alone and focus on, say, the other team's worst hitter. One Reddit contributor tells how he was at the park when a man with a batting average of .196 came to the plate. Fans broke into a mocking chant of "1-9-6! 1-9-6!," which may have ticked him off, because he promptly smashed a double against the center field fence. On his next at bat, in recognition of his new, improved batting average, the fans updated his stats but kept their derisive tone, chanting "1-9-8! 1-9-8!" He responded with a soaring home run. As he rounded the bases his teammates in the dugout began a chant of their own: "2-0-0! 2-0-0!" Okay, it may be time to hang up that heckle.

jogged out to take his position in the bottom of the eighth, the 34,010 fans at Fenway let him have it, en masse:

"Darrr-ryl . . . Darrr-ryl . . ."

The taunting was a sort of verbal sneer. It was like the way a playground bully teases you when you're a kid, only it wasn't one person doing the teasing; there were thousands and they kept repeating it:

"Darrr-ryl . . . Darrr-ryl . . . Darrr-ryl . . ."

Again and again and again they chanted his name and Strawberry, as rattled as Johnny Cueto would be a quarter of a century later, made matters worse by doffing his cap to the crowd. Intending this as a show of strength—*You can't hurt me*—it was in truth the opposite and everyone in the park knew it. They had done it. They had done what all hecklers and fans try to do to an opposing player. They had gotten to him.

"It's kind of lonely out there in right field," said broadcaster Vin Scully, describing

"Darrr-ryl . . .
Darrr-ryl . . ."

this scene to millions of viewers on national TV. "Boy, they're really on his case. I tell you what, if you don't want to live in a goldfish bowl, you better not be a big league ballplayer."

The Mets lost, and the series shifted back to New York for Game 6 with the Red Sox needing only one win to claim their first World Series in more than a half century. ("Nineteen eighteen," the last year the Red Sox won the title before their recent run of championships, was a frequent crowd chant when they came to New York.) On the hill for the Red Sox was their ace, Roger Clemens, the hard-throwing 24-game winner who would later win both the Cy Young and Most Valuable Player awards for that season. But he too found out what life was like in the goldfish bowl when Shea Stadium fans, doing to him what Boston's fans had done to their guy, chanted:

"Ro-gerrr . . . Ro-gerrr . . . Ro-gerrr . . ."

When Clemens left the game, in the seventh, Boston was leading, only to have New York tie it up in the eighth and eventually send it into extra innings. The Red Sox scored two in the top of the 10th, making it 5–3 and leaving the Mets for dead. Not so fast. New York came back in the bottom half of the inning to score three runs on a two-out rally and pull out a miracle win full of heroes, villains, and scapegoats of epic proportions.

Despite playing with an injured leg, Red Sox first baseman Bill Buckner made a catastrophic fielding error in that fateful 10th, an error that caused him to be the butt of jokes, heckling, cruelty, and even death threats from the very same fans who had been cheering him earlier. Stung by their loss, the Red Sox released him the next season, though he returned to play

> ## "If you don't want to live in a goldfish bowl, you better not be a big league ballplayer."

briefly for the club years later in the last season of a long, distinguished career.

Things ended more happily for the Mets, who beat the Red Sox in Game 7 to win their first World Series since the amazin' days of Tom Seaver. And the happiest man of all in their champagne-soaked clubhouse was Darryl Strawberry. Nobody was taunting him now.

CHAPTER 4

Showdown in the Garden:
Reggie v. Spike

Much has changed in sports since 1986, and for hecklers all these changes have been pretty damned good. There was no Internet back then; today there is a vast online world where you can post videos of yourself heckling LeBron or A-Rod or Tom Brady. These videos, shot on your smart phone by your girlfriend, your boyfriend, or a buddy whose laughter can be heard in the background, can be shared around the world on YouTube, Twitter, and other sites and—here is the most awesome thing of all—you don't even have to leave your seat at the game to go viral.

Except for a few colorful baseball cranks like Hilda Chester, late of Ebbets Field and the Brooklyn Dodgers, hecklers were basically anonymous in the old days. They shouted things at the park during the game, and when the game was over everybody went home and that was the end of it. A heckler was as memorable as the guy selling you peanuts or beer. You didn't pay any more attention to him than you needed to, unless he was really irritating and creeped you out or he was really entertaining and cracked you up. Then you noticed him. And while all of this is still mostly true about hecklers, there is one very notable exception:

Spike Lee.

Spike Lee, New York Knicks celebrity heckler.

Spike Lee is a celebrity who heckles or a heckler who is a celebrity, or perhaps both. In any case he is an identifiable presence at every game he attends and someone fans watch for as they watch the players on the court. He is a bigger name than many of those players and sometimes more entertaining as well.

His home floor is Madison Square Garden in New York City, and his team is the New York Knicks. Many Knicks fans admire Lee because he has authentic Brooklyn street cred, he's a hard-core devotee of ball, and he's as crazy about his Knicks as cowbell-clanging Hilda was about her beloved Bums.

Jack Nicholson, The Heckler

Jack Nicholson may have played The Joker in the movies, but sometimes at Lakers games he played another role: The Heckler.

The three-time Academy Award–winning star of such fine, still eminently watchable films as *Chinatown* and *Terms of Endearment*—not to mention his brilliant, comically maniacal performance in Tim Burton's *Batman*—Nicholson was a courtside fixture at the Fabulous Forum in Ingleside during the 1980s Showtime era of the Los Angeles Lakers. As a former high school player who really knew the game and loved it, he developed what one biographer called an "obsessive attachment" to the Lakers, particularly in their quest to beat their archrivals, the Boston Celtics. Another biographer, Patrick McGilligan, described the actor's volatile moods during games of this period: "There, for most of the major Lakers games, was Jack Nicholson, sitting with his arms calmly folded, hitting his forehead with his hand, or at times screaming at the referees."

To Nicholson's credit, just like Spike Lee, he did not just watch from the comfort and safety of his home arena; for the biggest games he ventured into the enemy's lair, and for the Celtics that meant Boston Garden. Mostly fans there welcomed him graciously, and he gladly signed autographs and posed for photographs with them. But when the game began in earnest, the good feelings came to a halt. In all their long and mostly successful years in the league, the Lakers had never beaten the Celtics in the NBA Finals until 1984, when they did it in six games. The clincher that year took place at Boston Garden, and Nicholson was on hand to rub it in. When the TV camera focused on him in his seat, as it always did a few times every game, he grinned his movie star grin and held up four fingers, signifying four wins and the end of Boston dominance over L.A.

Non-Knicks fans, however, tend to regard him as a major pain. Love him or despise him, as the saying goes, you cannot ignore him.

His seats are courtside at the Garden, which makes him pretty much impossible to ignore even if you try to. If he and his wife cannot attend one night, he will give his tickets to friends or family to make sure somebody fills his seats. For games he frequently suits up in a Knicks jersey, just like the players he has come to root for, throwing it on over a long-sleeve undershirt or sweater in cold weather. The undershirt is blue so as to fit in with the Knicks' blue and orange colors.

Jack Nicholson once mooned Boston Garden.

After another game at Boston Garden, one that ended with a hard Laker loss, Nicholson was so pissed at Celtic fans and their taunting of his team that he dropped his trousers and mooned the crowd. Boston's Hall of Fame coach and general manager Red Auerbach saw the stunt and was appalled. "I've seen a lot of fans in my day," he said, "and to me there's a difference between being an a** and being a fan." That was one time when people saw both the fan and the fan's a**.

Other times you might see him in a knit cap and jacket emblazoned with team logos. He also wears shoes and merchandise branded by Nike, with whom he has a business relationship, as well as T-shirts and caps that promote his latest Spike Lee Joint. Geek glasses are as much a part of his look as his mustache and goatee. Unlike the giants who race up and down the court in front of him, he is not a tall man.

Everybody knows Spike or knows of him—the players, coaches, media, refs, league officials, security—and he is on a first-name basis with the reigning superstars of the game. But unlike some celebs who show up just to get their faces on TV or purely to promote something, Spike is into it. Born in 1957, he became a Knicks fan as a boy, sneaking into the Garden to watch the Walt Frazier–Bill Bradley–Willis Reed clubs of that era win two NBA titles. All these decades later he still bleeds orange and blue, ecstatic when they win, depressed when they lose. And he knows The Game too. That's what he calls it: The Game. For him it is the best. He is a true fan—and a true heckler too.

Given that he is a filmmaker, fittingly Lee began his basketball heckling career in the movies—in his first feature film, *She's Gotta Have It*, which he wrote, directed, and acted in, playing a wise-talking character named Mars Blackmon who is Lee's alter ego. In the film Mars is having a conversation about basketball with a friend, and they are talking about a real NBA game—one in which Bernard King, a guard with the Knicks, went off against the Larry Bird–led Boston Celtics.

"'Nard was serving the whole Celtic squad," says Mars/Spike. "He even jammed Bird's ugly mug, a vicious death-defying Brooklyn Bridge high-flying 360 slam dunk." His friend then protests his characterization of Bird: "The white boy is bad and you got to give him credit. Larry Bird is the best player in the NBA." Mars/Spike isn't conceding anything, though, replying that Bird is "the ugliest motherf**ker in the NBA, that's what he is."

She's Gotta Have It became a surprise hit and heralded the young director's arrival as a moviemaker of note. Less pleased about Lee's success was Bird, who probably did not see the film but nonetheless heard about how he had been trashed in it. Ever since then the retired Celtics great, an Indiana Pacers executive since 1992, has remained cool and standoffish to Lee whenever their paths happen to cross.

During the 1980s, Bird's time in the basketball sun, he led the Celtics to three world titles, collected a roomful of individual trophies, and along with Magic Johnson is credited with bringing the NBA back to life when, in terms of fan and media interest and overall hipness, it was barely breathing. Lee's Knicks were mostly awful during this period, so it may be that Bird doesn't need to say anything.

Over the years, as Lee's success has grown—his next picture, *Do the Right Thing*, won him an Academy Award nomination, and he has since made many hit movies, documentaries, and commercials—his view in the Garden has improved from "the green seats to the yellow, to the red, then down to the floor," as he says. And now that he's courtside his heckling makes him no longer just a mere spectator at the game but sometimes part of it, pissing off visiting players and referees.

Detroit Piston Bad Boy Rick Mahorn once threw a ball at him during warm-ups. It hit him in the head and knocked his glasses off. Lee later described this as "inadvertent." Definitely not inadvertent was the time Scottie Pippen of the Chicago

Bulls threw down a monster dunk over Knicks center Patrick Ewing, causing the 7-footer to fall to the floor. When Pippen, in full badass mode, stood menacingly over Ewing lying on his back, Lee jumped to his feet and started yelling for the referee to call a technical foul on Pippen for taunting.

The 6-foot-8 Bulls forward walked over to him and said, "Sit the f**k down, Spike."

Except for Pippen, whom he has called "mean-spirited," Lee says he has good relations with players and that his heckling for the most part is taken in the spirit in which it is intended: fun, fair sport, part of the game. This is true too for the referees, to whom he targets the bulk of his criticism. When he asks refs, for instance, "How can you call that?" they may respond,

More celebrity heckler sightings

Rapper Kendrick Lamar is straight outta Compton, and like Jack Nicholson he became a passionate fan of the hometown team, so passionate that during one game against Oklahoma City at the Staples Center in downtown Los Angeles he just could not shut up. Every time the Thunder came down the floor he had something to say from his courtside seat.

Finally one fan couldn't take it anymore. With Kevin Durant on the free throw line and the arena momentarily quiet, he shouted, "Hey Kendrick, woe is me. You got something to say. Every play! Shut up!" Durant heard the heckler clearly, as did everyone else in the vicinity, and he smiled broadly and laughed.

It is probably not right to describe the girlfriends of NBA stars as celebrities, although some of them almost qualify. One time Chris Bosch's girlfriend—this was when Bosch was on the Toronto Raptors—was talking smack about LeBron James when LeBron was playing for Cleveland the first time. All game long Bosch's girlfriend and another woman were yapping at James, who could do nothing early on. But with the ladies pulling a Kendrick and not shutting up, he started to do everything, filling up the hole like only he can and leading the visiting Cavs to a win. Asked about the women in a postgame interview, James said, "Yeah, they're the reason the Raptors lost tonight. They ticked me off a little bit."

So it goes with hecklers. Just ask Spike Lee. Sometimes your team wins, and sometimes you piss the other guys off so much your team leaves the court with an L.

with a laugh, "Don't ask if you don't know." Another time a ref blew his whistle on the Knicks for a zone violation that no one, players and coaches included, had ever seen before. When Spike popped off about it, the ref explained, "I gotta call it once a year and this is it." Lee shook his head and sat back down.

There was one extraordinary incident, however, when Spike's heckling turned against him and the team he loves. It might be called The Reggie Miller Game—or more properly, The Game in which Reggie Plunged a Spike into the Heart of Spike Lee, for this was when Miller, now a TV broadcaster but then a deadly accurate three-point shooter for the Indiana Pacers, single-handedly destroyed the Knicks in Game 5 of the 1994 Eastern Conference Finals at Madison Square Garden. Here is a blow-by-blow account of the destruction:

- Fourth quarter begins. With the series tied at two games apiece, the Knicks are sailing along, leading 70–58, and have the game well in hand. Even better for them, Reggie Miller, the Pacers' one and only scoring threat, is tanking. Can't do anything right. This gives Spike Lee an idea: "I began to get on Reggie, just a little," he recalls in his basketball memoir *Best Seat in the House*.

- Perhaps in response, or perhaps just because he was overdue, the Pacers' long and lanky shooting guard buries a three to open the quarter. This stirs up more trash talk from Lee, who is "still having fun." Lee's idea of fun, however, consists of him yelling at the Knick guards to get up in Reggie's grill more, put their hands on him, get physical. Spike also screams at the referees to call the moving screens that he claims the Pacers are setting to free up Reggie for his shots.

- Needless to say, the object of his taunts does not take kindly to any of this, and the next time down the floor he hits another long-range bomb. Suddenly the Knicks' once-comfortable lead is down to six, and the bomb-thrower turns directly to Lee and glares at him.

- But Lee does not take the hint and keeps yelling at him: "I got caught up. I yelled back," Lee admits. "It was like Reggie was playing me as well as the Knicks. He pointed at me. He gestured. I pointed back at him. 'Let's get on this guy!' I screamed." Clearly Reggie feels the same way, because after sinking a two-pointer to pull the Pacers to within four with 9:08 left, he runs back on defense and glares at Lee the whole way. Now the TV broadcast has caught up with the psychodrama occurring on the Garden floor, and the cameras follow Miller's taunting of Lee after every shot he makes.

- Two more minutes elapse, and suddenly the Knicks' 12-point lead to start the quarter is gone. Score is tied. And then Reggie hits another that finds nothing but net and the Pacers are in the lead. As he does so he points to his chest and stares over at a certain somebody with "a De Niroesque scowl," as that certain somebody described it.

- Now there is 5:52 on the clock and the Pacers lead by eight! And Reggie is gesturing anew to Spike, putting both hands around his throat and making the choke sign. What makes this extra sweet for Reggie is that he is doing all this damage while being guarded—if that's the right term; it's more like he is being chased ineffectually around the court—by Knicks guard John Starks, who is Lee's favorite player. But even at this late juncture, when all is collapsing around him, Lee cannot sit still, bouncing up to tell the refs that Miller should be T-ed up for taunting. "I don't think Spike realizes that he's not in the game," says broadcaster Marv Albert drily over the air.

Reggie Miller to Spike Lee
and his Knicks.

Lee's boys did make a run of it and tightened things up for a while, but the Pacers pulled away again and won handily. The reason for the Indiana win was, in Albert's accurate assessment, "an astounding shooting exhibition" by Miller, who scored 37 points overall, 25 in that deciding fourth quarter, and got off an All-Star one-liner. Asked in a postgame courtside interview about Spike Lee, he smiled and said, "Spike who?"

Later, in a press conference, he expanded his remarks somewhat, saying that "sometimes he [Spike] opens his mouth a little bit too much and gets the other guys going. Tonight was one of those nights." Indeed it was and everyone, including Spike, who buried his head in his hands at game's end, knew it.

"Spike Lee lost the game; he got Reggie pissed off," said Bob Gutkowski, president of Madison Square Garden, expressing the sentiments of many New Yorkers. "THANKS A LOT, SPIKE," shouted the headline in the New York Daily News, while the Post was more succinct: "SPIKED!" Talk radio blasted him, and the Daily News ran a readers' poll asking whether he should be allowed to sit courtside if the series returned to New York for Game 7. A reporter even brought up the controversy with Mayor Rudy Giuliani, who said Lee should be able to express his opinions at a game in the grand tradition of American sports. Some Knicks even stopped Lee's sister on the street to tell her that her brother should stay away.

But a Game 7, at this point, was merely a hypothetical. The Knicks had lost the fifth game at home. The Pacers were now leading three games to two, and the series was shifting back to Indiana for Game 6, where a win by the Pacers would deliver them to the NBA Finals and crush the Knicks. Making things worse for Lee—as he prepared to fly to Indianapolis to see the game—was the knowledge that he had committed the one unpardonable sin that no heckler or fan ever wants to: He had hurt his team.

"THANKS A LOT, SPIKE!"

CHAPTER 5

The greatest sixth man in basketball history

In describing his feelings for the New York Knicks at the time, Reggie Miller spoke with the same blunt honesty he had showed in his on-court confrontation with Spike Lee. "I'm telling you right now I hate the Knicks," he said. "Absolutely hate those kids." When asked *why* he felt so strongly, he spoke about the previous year's playoffs in which those New York kids met the Pacers in the first round of a five-game series beginning at the Garden. From the opening tip their strategy was clear: Beat on Indiana's best player and make his life miserable. On the first two plays of the game John Starks hit Miller hard twice, drawing two fouls, and after the second foul Starks called him a "bitch." "First of all," Reggie said, "you don't ever call me 'bitch.' I call you that. That's my game."

These were fighting words to Miller, who started oiling up his jump shot. He went on a scoring frenzy and at one point he glanced up at the scoreboard and then to the Knicks guard, saying, "Miller 26, Starks 5. You ever gonna score tonight?" Starks may not have scored much, but his teammates did and Miller and Indiana lost that game and the next in New York.

For Game 3, at Market Square Arena in Indianapolis, Starks became so frustrated with Miller that he head-butted him. The referee rung him up for a flagrant foul and ejected him. Meanwhile Reggie kept scoring and

"You ever gonna score tonight?"

openly trashed the Knicks players. "You bitches aren't as tough as everybody says you are," he told them as he led the Pacers to a win. The Knicks nevertheless regained their footing and closed out Indiana in the next game (it was a best-of-five series then), setting up the high-stakes, bad blood rematch that was the 1994 Eastern Conference finals. When Spike Lee, suddenly part of the story of the series, arrived in Indianapolis for Game 6, he still wasn't sure what hit him. "Reggie is raining profanities upon my ears," he wrote later. "He's calling me everything but a child of God. He gives me the choke sign with his hand and grabs his crotch with his other hand."

What was he supposed to do, given these provocations? What would anyone do? Many a heckler would respond the same way: "I wasn't going to sit like a bump on a log, so I began to yell back," Lee recalled.

Securing his status as the Pacers' Public Enemy No. 1—a status that Knicks fans had also bestowed upon him—the

Indianapolis Star printed Spike Lee paper cutout masks for fans to wear at the game. (A Detroit paper had done the same thing with Jack Nicholson at the Silverdome during the heated Lakers-Pistons rivalry a few years earlier.) Even so the object of their scorn bravely took a seat courtside for Game 6 and cheered his boys onto a tough but gratifying beat-down of the Pacers, 98–91. He and another figure of derision, John Starks, who helped cool Miller off with hard but fair defense, hugged afterward on the court. Lee needed security to exit the arena. "It was a completely hostile crowd, didn't seem to be that far from actual violence, and I kid you not," he said.

The Knicks' win returned the series to New York, where they nailed down the final game and moved on to the NBA Finals (losing to Houston in another tough seven-gamer). Vanquished once again by his bitter rivals, an utterly spent Reggie Miller cried in the locker room. It was left for him to wait one more year before he and the Pacers could finally slay the New York dragon, outlasting the Knicks in the 1995 conference semifinals in yet another grueling seven-game series replete with ill will and fire-breathing drama. (Indiana lost in the next round, however.) After all this Lee and Miller eventually patched up their differences, as Lee wrote the preface to Miller's book *I Love Being the Enemy*. As an NBA analyst for TNT, Miller broadcasts Knicks games from time to time in New York, and when he's there he no longer flashes the choke sign to his former nemesis when he sees him popping up, as usual, to protest some call from his seat on the floor of the Garden. And for the most part New York hoop fans have forgiven Spike for his playoff excesses of long ago.

The other lead actor in this drama within a drama was John Starks. Despite his problems guarding Reggie, he remains a hero to Knicks fans, including Lee, for being a hard-working, pull-yourself-up-by-your-bootstraps overachiever, which New Yorkers like, and for never giving up, which they like even more. Now retired from active play and a community relations advisor with the team, he too no longer has a beef with Reggie and thinks all the Lee-taunting-Miller stuff was overblown anyway.

"It's part of the game," he told blogger Henry Abbott. "Fans. The interaction. That's the beauty of basketball. More so than any other sport. Fans have that close relationship with the players. So you get a lot of back-and-forth conversations."

Of all the professional team sports, only in basketball do fans sit so close to the action with nothing between them and the players. In baseball you're farther away, and in football and soccer you're farther away still. Glass walls protect hockey fans from errant pucks but also form a barrier between players and spectators. No such glass barrier exists in tennis, but even the fans who sit courtside are still set back from the players. In golf—not a "team sport" except at the Ryder Cup and similar matches—fans sometimes stand so close to the players that they can reach out and touch them—a no-no in all sports, and a sure way to get tossed.

Like many players in all sports, past and present, Starks believes that heckling "sometimes can be motivating. It can get a particular guy going." He also believes that it can be effective—that it can get inside a guy's head and mess with him. "For some other players, it can take them out of the game because they're so focused on what that fan is doing."

The NBA's Fan Code of Conduct puts limits on what hecklers can say and do, and the league will warn those whose behavior it regards as out of line and in extreme cases—such as the fan who was hassling Carmelo Anthony at the Garden—eject them. Richard Anderson is a professor of ophthalmology at the University of Utah and a Salt Lake City surgeon who has earned the nickname of "Dr. Heckle" for his years of heckling behind the basket at Utah Jazz games. As committed to the Jazz as Lee is to the Knicks, he has expressed this commitment by painting team insignia on his face, wearing costumes, blowing a saxophone while an opposing player attempted

NBA Fan Code of Conduct

The NBA has apparently lifted a practice from soccer and is now issuing red cards. But the red cards are not for players who have committed egregious fouls, as they are in soccer, but to unruly fans. Here is what the warning card says:

"You are being issued a warning that the comments, gestures and/or behaviors that you have directed at players, coaches, game officials and/or other spectators constitute excessive verbal abuse and are in violation of the NBA Fan Code of Conduct. This is the first and only warning that you will receive. If, after receiving this warning, you verbally abuse any player, coach, game official or spectator, you will be immediately ejected from the arena without refund."

ESPN's Keith Olbermann reported that although the cards have been in existence since 2005—likely in response to the Malice in the Palace the year before—they are very seldom used. Olbermann could find only one instance in which the league had actually red-carded a fan. But the NBA Fan Code of Conduct remains in effect, and the league and teams have shown that they will enforce it when necessary.

The code is posted on team and arena websites. Setting forth "standards of decorum" that fans must adhere to, it says that "guests will enjoy the basketball experience free from disruptive behavior, including foul or abusive language or obscene gestures." Nor are "any obscene or indecent messages on signs or clothing" permitted. Fans must drink responsibly, and if they "engage in fighting, throwing objects or attempting to enter the court," they will be tossed from the game. The NBA encourages fans to report "any inappropriate behavior" to ushers and security officials who can then take the necessary actions. Besides being ejected from the game, misbehaving fans can have their season tickets revoked and be subject to possible arrest and prosecution.

a free throw (the ref confiscated the sax shortly thereafter), waving blow-up dolls and a rubber chicken (the ref nabbed that one too), and yelling through a hollowed-out Coke cup or megaphone or a purple-painted parking cone everything he can think of that's not profane or in poor taste that will mess with Utah's opponents.

As well known to Salt Lake fans, in his way, as the team mascot, Jazz Bear, Dr. Heckle unveiled an umbrella at a game a couple of years ago at Energy Solutions Arena in Salt Lake, spinning it around like he was taking a Sunday stroll in the park as LeBron James, then of the Miami Heat, stood on the line shooting a pair of free throws. Wrong move evidently, because NBA officials told him to cease and desist with the umbrella and other props. A Jazz season ticket holder for decades, Anderson had done similar things in the past and only rarely had anyone said anything against it. He accused the league of trying to shut him up in order to protect James. At the next Jazz game, after the superstar had left town, Anderson sat in his familiar seat behind the basket and wore blue masking tape over his mouth, a silent protest against what he regarded as an NBA gag order.

But he removed the tape long enough to blast the league to a television reporter, saying that "the commissioner and the NBA central office have taken control of who they want to win and who makes them the most money. What really upset them was when I was twirling my umbrella when LeBron James was shooting free throws. If it was one of our guys in a different arena, probably they wouldn't have cared so much about it."

The NBA's sensitivity on the issue of fan behavior stems from a variety of reasons. One is the physical closeness

Richard "Dr. Heckle" Anderson in silent protest against the NBA.

between fans and players. Another is the infamous Malice in the Palace brawl and other player-fan incidents in which that closeness, generally a plus for basketball, turns negative when the invisible walls of separation break down. One more reason is the gripe that people come to see supremely gifted talents such as James, not to see hecklers.

There is yet another reason why hecklers annoy the hell out of the NBA. His name is Robin Ficker.

Encore John Starks, recalling the days when he was starring for the Knicks: "I can remember the fan in Washington D.C., he'd always sit behind the bench. He was a lawyer. He always gave us grief. He looked forward to getting on players. He knew your whole background . . . everything. It was just a lot of fun."

The man he is referring to is Ficker. Now let's turn to Spike Lee, who did not regard Ficker as fun but rather as "the leather-lunged madman down in Washington." Red Auerbach of the Boston Celtics argued that Ficker was "a disgrace" to basketball and that his season tickets should be stripped from him. (This was due to Ficker's relentless haranguing of two Celtic mainstays, Larry Bird and Kevin McHale, calling them "Larry Nerd" and "Kevin McSnail," among other things.) Then there is John Salley, center for the Detroit Pistons (and now a TV personality), who often lined up against Bird and McHale. Ficker harangued him pretty good too. His opinion?

"He was the heckler of all hecklers," said Smalley. "He didn't cross the line. He just disrupted the squad."

Disruption was indeed the name of the game for the man who is widely regarded as the LeBron James or Michael Jordan of heckling. Not a big man but physically fit with glasses and cropped hair, Ficker graduated from the University of Baltimore School of Law and obtained a BS in electrical and mechanical engineering from Case Institute of Technology. A Maryland attorney since the early 1970s, he had argued in front of the U.S. District Court, and one of his cases, which challenged the NFL's blackout rule that barred local games from being televised if the home team's stadium did not sell out, went all the way to the Supreme Court. As a lawyer he wielded his voice with authority, and it proved to be a blunt-force instrument in heckling too.

His team, the team he loved and cheered for, was the Washington Bullets (now the Wizards), who played their home games in Landover, Maryland, a short commute from where Ficker lived. His heckling debut occurred in 1986, the same year chants of "Darrr-ryl" rocked Fenway. But when he showed up for the first time to root on the Bullets and root against whomever they were playing, he did not sit in the cheap seats and hope against hope that the opposing team would hear him. No, he *made sure* of it, buying two season tickets behind the visitors' bench. Not to the left or right of it but directly

Robin Ficker has been called the "heckler of all hecklers."

behind it. So close he could have handed the players towels or cups of Gatorade when they came off the floor during time-outs. It was during those time-outs that Ficker did his greatest damage as a heckler, tearing into the opposing team at the worst possible moments for them: when the coach was trying to talk to his players.

But—and this was only one of the ways in which he lifted the ancient art of heckling, as sportscasters like to say, to a whole new level—he always worked smart. Raw, unfiltered, idiotic drivel did not spew as if from a broken sewer main from his lips, as it does with so many lesser talents. He never drank. He never cursed. He never made remarks about race or sex. He never said anything about children. What he did instead was to fall back on what he did as an attorney when preparing for trial: research, research, research. Armed with this information Ficker did not just heckle opposing players, he cross-examined them.

This was, mind you, in that primitive era before smartphones, wi-fi connected arenas, and instantaneous Googling of a player's rap sheet. Ficker did his research the old-fashioned way, reading newspapers, magazines, and books to compile the information he needed to make his case not in front of The Bench but behind it. "I tried to make it fun," he told *USA Today*. "There is such a thing as a home-court advantage—the sixth man in basketball, the 12th man in football."

And so, that is what he became—the greatest nonplaying sixth man in the history of basketball. Here are his top 10 greatest heckling moments, counting down from No. 10.

10. Jason Kidd, then a point guard with the Dallas Mavericks, showed up to play the Bullets on their home floor and

Quotations from Chairman Robin

Robin Ficker, the best there ever was, on heckling:

James Harden models proper heckling protective gear.

- "A heckler is someone who tries to take the mind of the opponent off their game, get them thinking about someone else, something the coach isn't telling them, anything other than what they're supposed to be doing, anything other than their opponent."

- "I wasn't drinking alcohol. I never used profanity. Never made any racial or sexual comments. I never said anything that couldn't be printed in the paper. I did have a robust discussion of the issues."

- "There is such a thing as the First Amendment. These guys are paid a lot to focus on what they're supposed to be doing for a few hours."

- "Fans who don't know the bounds of their conduct should be held responsible for whatever happens—and should also be barred from future games."

- "Fans who want to distract players need to use brains, not brawn, and employ a little bit of armchair psychology."

- "Words are enough to cause the opposition to lose concentration."

- "Put in earplugs or cotton balls. I've had NBA players do that." (His advice to players who don't want to be heckled.)

- "You're not gonna be great unless you think you are great."

Ficker, strangely, was standing behind the bench, holding a sign that read ASON.

This was strange because Kidd, a superb passer and play-maker who struggled with his outside shooting, had no idea why. He stared at the sign with a puzzled expression, unable to figure it out. Finally he had to ask what it meant and Ficker said, "Because you have no J."

9. Vernon Maxwell of the Houston Rockets had a hot tem-per, chasing a Portland heckler into the stands and punching him in the face. The next time Maxwell and the Rockets played against the Bullets, Ficker sat behind Houston's bench wearing a baseball catcher's mask.

8. In an article evaluating the sartorial habits of NBA coaches, *USA Today* rated Frank Layden of the Utah Jazz as the worst dressed in the league. When Ficker chose to point this out to Layden, with extreme redundancy, the Jazz coach "tried to come through the seats after me," Ficker recalled. Layden did not reach him, but on another occasion he successfully spit on him. LaSalle Thompson of the Indiana Pacers did too.

7. In his prime, Los Angeles Lakers center Shaquille O'Neal rapped on several hip-hop records, boasting in one song, "I've got skills." Ficker bought the record, listened to the rap, rewrote the words a la Weird Al Yankovic, and then sang a parody ver-sion to O'Neal on the Lakers bench, changing the lyrics to "You've got bills."

6. Pro athletes have been known to meet women on the road and father children with them, not getting involved in their lives except to pay child support to the mothers. One such player was Lewis Lloyd, a fast-living forward for the Rockets. As Ficker tells it, when he "reminded" Lloyd of his

"delinquent child support payments," it rattled him completely and threw him off his game.

5. In a similar tactic, when the Chicago Bulls came to town, Ficker recited all the names of Scottie Pippen's ex-girlfriends—by all accounts, a very long list. (He married in 1997.) One can only guess how the star forward responded, but as Robin has said, opposing players and coaches often referred to him using "many F-words besides Ficker."

4. The coach for the Bulls in their Jordan-Pippen championship years of the 1990s was Phil Jackson, who penned an autobiography, *Maverick*, in which he discussed some of his own sexual dalliances. Ficker bought the book, brought it to the game, and in his most commanding legal tone, read the most salacious parts aloud. Said Ficker, "Phil was getting mad at me for reading what he wrote. I told him if he was that mad about it, he shouldn't have written it."

3. Isaiah Thomas once threw a shoe, not in jest, at him. Others pitched water at him. One player hit him in the face with a wet towel and Ficker responded, "That's the only thing you've hit all night." Back in the days when Don Nelson was coaching Golden State and his son Donnie, now an executive with the Dallas Mavericks, was his baby-faced assistant, Ficker homed in on the younger Nelson and teased him mercilessly, saying, "Little Donnie, you go to sleep like a baby after this game. You're gonna wake up every two hours and cry." Golden State players later doused Ficker with a bucket of Gatorade.

2. Charles Barkley was another favorite target. While starring for the Philadelphia 76ers and Phoenix Suns, Barkley had several angry run-ins with fans, including accidentally spitting on a young girl when he was aiming at a heckler who had been

bothering him. (He later apologized to the girl and her family.) Ficker nailed him for this, and that, and this, and that, until Barkley announced he was thinking about running for senator or governor in his home state of Alabama after he retired from basketball.

"Charles," said Ficker, "before I vote for you, I want to know what your views are on the economy, NAFTA, and health care."

"I do have a view about the death penalty. They should use it on you," said Barkley, striking a blow for all his fellow players who had been tortured by Ficker over the years.

1. No one was spared Ficker's barbs, not even Michael Jordan, who reportedly once chucked a basketball at him. The Bulls superstar frequented casinos and bet tens of thousands of dollars on golf. One of his gambling and golf partners wrote an unauthorized tell-all book about it, and Ficker read passages from it behind the Bulls bench. He also brought oversize gambling dice and playing cards and continually asked, "Hey Michael, wanna bet?" Despite their differences Charles Barkley so admired Ficker's work that he brought him to Phoenix to heckle Jordan for the 1993 NBA Finals between Barkley's Suns and the Bulls. Barkley paid Ficker's airfare and got him a seat at America West Arena in his customary spot behind the visiting team's bench. Clad in a Bullets "You Gotta Believe"

Ficker shook a yellow rubber chicken at Jordan.

T-shirt and a white Suns ball cap, Ficker shook a yellow rubber chicken at Jordan and goaded him about his gambling. It had little effect, though, as the Bulls whipped the Suns twice in Phoenix and easily won their third straight NBA title.

Many in the NBA, including some Washington fans, hated Ficker's act and lobbied team owner Abe Pollin to revoke his season tickets. This was not so easily done, however. An accomplished attorney who knew his way around a court-room, Ficker believed strongly that heckling was a right pro-tected by the First Amendment of the Constitution. "I think it's appropriate to exercise your free speech rights at an athletic contest," he said. "I don't think there's anything wrong with using a booming voice at a wrestling match or a football game or a basketball game. People should be able to let loose and have a little fun."

Another thing working in his favor, fair or not, was the widely held public sentiment that pro athletes are spoiled, overpaid brats. "An athlete making more for playing a single game than the average American makes in a year should be able to withstand the slings and arrows of a fan's remarks or even a beer shower," Ficker wrote in an opinion piece for the *New York Times*.

Nevertheless, in 1997, after more than a decade of slinging those arrows, he decided to no longer buy season tickets and to stop attending NBA games. The reason was that in Decem-ber of that year Washington was moving to a new arena, and when this occurred he would no longer be allowed to purchase seats behind the visitors' bench. If he wished to he could buy tickets behind one of the baskets, far away from where he had harassed opposing teams. He declined the offer.

Wizards management said it was forced to make this move to comply with federal regulations that required providing

Fans violating the NBA's Ficker Rule, which prohibits interfering with coach-player communication during time-outs.

access to the disabled at the new arena. Ficker thought this was ludicrous and protested the move in a letter to Pollin. "I love the NBA players but not the owners," he said.

Although this brought his heckling career to an end, his imprint on the game endures. The NBA passed what has come to be known as "the Ficker Rule," which states that fans cannot interfere with communications between a coach and players during a time-out. The back of every season ticket application contains language to this effect that fans must agree to when purchasing tickets.

Since saying good-bye to the NBA, Ficker has continued to work as an attorney, stayed active politically, run for office in his home Maryland district, and become an ardent supporter of the University of Maryland wrestling squad. Whenever some nasty piece of business surfaces in sports, such as player vs. fan violence, the media will search him out to hear his thoughts on what it means when one, or both, of the two camps "crosses the line."

A few years ago, purely for kicks, he appeared as a guest on an afternoon TV show hosted by Jeff Probst of *Survivor* fame. Also for yuks, Isaiah Thomas posed as a member of the studio audience and heckled Ficker as he was being interviewed and then, in a nod to bygone days, tossed a shoe at him. It sailed far over Ficker's head and didn't come close to hitting him, unlike the old days when Thomas really meant it.

When called up on stage, Isaiah, flashing his million-dollar smile and looking like money in a gold suit, exchanged a good-natured shake and a bro hug with his former antagonist. Probst asked Ficker if heckling superstars like Thomas ever made him nervous. Ficker smiled and said that although Isaiah was one of the best guards ever, "there were lots of ways he could improve his game and I made those suggestions to him."

Such as?

"Well, I would say to Isaiah, there are three kinds of point guards. There are point guards that make things happen, there are point guards that watch things happen, and there are point guards like you who don't know what's happening."

Everyone shared a good laugh over this, including Isaiah, and it again showed the truth of the old adage about how time heals all wounds, even for hecklers and their prey.

CHAPTER 6

Walking the runway

Robin Ficker did his heckling and cheering behind the opposing team's bench. Spike Lee yaks at refs and players courtside. Dr. Heckle twirled his umbrella behind one of the baskets. All are splendid vantage points from which to unloose verbal sallies for one essential reason: The players can hear you.

Each of these men occupied seats where they could be heard—an obvious element of effective heckling. Here is another: quiet. With the advent of the Ficker Rule it is verboten to disturb coaches and players during a time-out. Not that anyone can be heard during an NBA timeout these days anyway, what with Taylor Swift and Eminem blasting from the sound system and promos and commercials playing on the scoreboard screens and cheerleaders and mascots doing their routines. This is why basketball hecklers today, like Brooklyn's

Mr. Whammy, focus on free throws—because they can potentially make a player miss during that brief moment when the arena has become relatively, and some might say blessedly, quiet.

In baseball there are many more lulls and lapses of activity and periods of relative quiet than in basketball, and this is why hecklers flourish there as well. They sit in the bleachers or around the bullpen and home plate area where players can also hear them.

Now we turn to football, America's most popular team sport but the least welcoming one for hecklers. Why is that? Why is it harder to heckle in the NFL than in the NBA, MLB, or NHL? In hockey there is the visitors' penalty box, where players from the opposing team must serve their punishment after committing a foul. They have no choice but to sit and listen to fans tell them how lousy they are and how much they suck. Being freed from "the sin bin," as it's called, lets players return to the ice and escape all that abuse.

But football has no penalty box, no bullpen, no free throw line. It is no small feat to even get within shouting distance of NFL players during a game. Fans are of course not allowed on the field except in special circumstances. Sometimes in college ball students will crash the barriers and swarm the field after a big win over a rival school. They frolic and gambol in delight and some gleefully taunt the losing players and coaches to make them feel even worse than they do. In situations like these students can walk right up to the players and go eye to eye with them, something fans of Andrew Luck or Aaron Rodgers can do after a game only if they are willing to be gang-tackled by security staff.

It may be that you have taken out a second mortgage on your home and popped for choice season tickets around the 50-yard line of your favorite team's stadium. Congrats bro, job well done. However, if you are entertaining thoughts of doing some heckling from this venue, good luck. Let's say you have field-level seats on the side where the visitors have their bench. Yes, you may able to shout annoying things to the guys who are not in the game, the guys who are mulling around the side-lines mostly with their butts facing you, who are wearing large padded helmets that make it hard to hear someone talking to them 5 feet away, let alone a person yelling at them from back in the stands. But what about the guys who are actually in the game? How do you heckle *them*?

They are the ones you need to get to, because they are the ones who are making the plays in the moment that will decide the game. All you need to do is lift your voice and send it soar-ing over that mass of bodies on the sideline so that it reaches the opposing team's quarterback, the man with the ball, who in all likelihood has a coach speaking into his ear inside his helmet. By saying just the right insulting thing at just the right moment, you cause him to stumble and lose control of the ball into the hands of one of your guys who, in an incredible game-changing turnabout, runs it all the way back for a TD. Although not one of the so-called experts on the postgame shows ever mentions your name, you know in your heart it was all because of you.

Then again, maybe not.

The end zone sections are the best places to heckle during a game. Lots of heavy hecklers and drinkers congregate there, standing and screaming and shouting obscenities all game

How to survive and thrive in the Black Hole

Oakland's Black Hole, says the *New York Times*, is "one of the toughest places for a team to play" in the NFL. The *Baltimore Sun* calls it "the scariest collection of fans" in football. TV analyst Shannon Sharpe, a former Denver Broncos tight end, said he'd "rather be in prison for a day" than go near the Black Hole when he was playing against the Raiders. "It's a lot safer."

The Black Hole is an end zone section on the lower deck of the south end of the O.co Coliseum. And like the Dawg Pound for the Cleveland Browns, it attracts a particularly avid type of fan—deeply loyal to the home team, intensely critical of their opponents. Heckling is encouraged.

Here are eight tips on how to survive and thrive in the Black Hole:

1. **Start partying the night before.** Ricky's Sports Theatre & Grill in nearby San Leandro is the Studio 54 or Elaine's of the Black Hole set.

2. **Start tailgating early.** After a hard night of partying, you'll be in the right frame of mind to begin a hard morning of partying in the parking lot hours before the game.

3. **Paint your face.** Raider colors are silver and black. Avoid pink pastels.

4. **Dress appropriately.** When choosing the right look for the Black Hole, imagine that you're auditioning for the next installment of the *Mad Max* movie series. Black is *de rigueur*. Goth is the right vibe. Skeleton masks and toy swords are good. So are spikes, chains, skulls on shoulder pads, hard hats, and Darth Vader apparel.

5. **Get a nickname.** Black Hole characters all have colorful nicknames such as Stoner Dude, Blitz Chick, Blitz Dude, Lord Mordred, Raider Maximus, and Spike. Those whose outfits feature skulls, and there are lots of them, are known as the Skull Patrol.

6. **Do not sit.** No one ever sits in the Black Hole. You must stand.

7. **Be loud.** Be very, very loud. It would not be right to recommend that you throw things at opposing players, although the Black Hole is known for it: batteries,

long. Their strength of numbers and sheer volume can make an impact on the game, although again, the noise in the stadium at large often drowns them out. And they are little more than costumed, face-painted bystanders when the action moves down the field away from them.

The gentle souls of the Raiders' Black Hole.

bottle caps, chicken bones, coins, golf balls, and cups of beer. A good prop is always welcome, such as a dummy with the jersey number of the opposing QB that you can beat up.

8. **Leave the delicate sensibilities at home.** If it's culture you want, go to a ballet. *Ladies Home Journal* writer Alysse Minkoff went on special assignment with a friend and watched a game from within the Black Hole. Her friend told her afterward that she had heard the F-word more times in a single day than she had her entire life, and that "she had never seen so many men grabbing themselves."

If the best place to heckle is the end zone, the best time to do it is before the game starts, during warm-ups, when the crowd is still filing in or sitting up in the mezzanine bars having drinks, and the players are tossing the ball around, practicing their kicks or whatever, and noise is less of an issue. When they get the chance, NFL hecklers can get as down and dirty as any fans anywhere. "They are verbalizing about your mother and your brother and your sister and your girlfriend, all during warm-ups," said Steve Mariucci, the former San Francisco 49ers coach who is now a TV commentator. "What are you supposed to do, charge the mound?" No, what you do is take it and try to turn it to your advantage, as

NFL hecklers can get as down and dirty as any fans any- where.

defensive tackle Steve McMichael did when he played for the Chicago Bears. "It can get nasty," he recalled, "but if you're getting trash-talked, it just motivates you to play harder."

One form of heckling that dominates football is tearing into anyone who shows up wearing the colors of the visitors. At a New England Patriots–New York Jets game at the Meadowlands, to cite only one example among many, a man in a Patriots jersey had the misfortune of walking past a Jets fan who welcomed him to New York as he climbed up some nearby steps: "You stink bubblehead. Your defense so sucks. You're gonna get outta New York. In your face, loser."

As the man kept walking, perhaps to find his seat or to flee the abuse, the fan kept after him, "In your face, in your face, in your face." Then, after the Jets scored a touchdown, the fan turned back to the man and started in again, "Hey look at that! In your face, shut your mouth, pay attention. In your face! I don't care wherever you are. Shut your mouth up."

This particular heckler happened to be a boy, seven years old, and his parents can be proud because at least he was using his words to express himself.

"This isn't a nice-guy league," Bill Parcells, the former New York Giants coach, was once quoted as saying, and the hecklers are not exactly warm and fuzzy either. TMZ aired a segment on heckling NFL quarterbacks at Super Bowl XLVII in New Orleans between the Baltimore Ravens and San Francisco 49ers. A heckler saw 49ers quarterback Colin Kaepernick on the street and ran after him saying, "Colin, when you get to the middle of the field, are you going to do heads or tails?"

Kaepernick just looked at him and said nothing, and TMZ's coverage jumped to another NFL quarterback cruising the streets of the Big Easy: journeyman Matt Leinart, who was in the last year of his career. TMZ's voiceover alluded to this, saying, "Hey look, it's a quarterback who used to be relevant—Matt Leinart!" Still, he was relevant enough to be approached by two Bourbon Street irregulars, who yelled "Matt Leinart sucks!" and "Hey, you f**ked up the Cardinals." Leinart's response mimicked Kaepernick's—keep walking, say nothing—and the TMZ crew stayed with him. "How you deal with that B.S., bro?" they asked. The former Heisman Trophy winner waved it gracefully away. "Just jealous haters, man," he said.

In its journalistic pursuit to get both sides of the story, TMZ went back to the jealous haters for a comment from them. "If Matt Leinart wants to continue playing sports," said one, "he should try softball."

So you can reach players during the game, sort of, and you can encounter guys on the street, maybe, or holler at them from behind a rope line as they parade by with their girlfriends

Heckling Roger Goodell

NFL Commissioner Roger Goodell is one of the most powerful men in sports and as such a figure ripe for heckling. There are good and not-so-good ways to do it, however, as these three case studies attest.

NOT SO GOOD

At a press conference at a New York City hotel to discuss his and the NFL's handling of the Ray Rice wife-beating incident and to announce a special investigation into the issue, Goodell was speaking when a heckler broke into the room hoping to disrupt the meeting. Not a chance, buddy. Security pounced on him and shoved him into an elevator as the frightened heckler screamed and tried to resist. He was gone in less than 60 seconds. Business returned to normal and Goodell, not a single strand of his carefully combed strawberry blond hair mussed, resumed taking questions. Officials no doubt ran a background check on the heckler before escorting him out of the hotel and possibly into a waiting NYPD squad car.

BETTER

In the Deflategate controversy, in which Goodell and the NFL charged Tom Brady and the New England Patriots with deliberately tampering with footballs in order to win the AFC title game, a New York federal court held a hearing to review the case. On the day of the hearing Goodell arrived in a black Cadillac Escalade that pulled up in front of the courthouse. As a man opened his door, Goodell stepped out of the SUV, buttoning his suit jacket and walking past a crowd of photographers and onlookers who had gathered to see him (and Tom Brady, who arrived moments later).

From somewhere in the crowd a man yelled, "People aren't stupid, Goodell. People aren't stupid. This is America." Another man shouted a single word and repeated it several times: "Lies!"

into some gala charity hotel ball, or perhaps see them as they get into their cars in the parking lot after a game. Still, it is not easy to get close to these guys, whatever the time or setting. Although many are household names and their games are seen by millions around the globe, in some ways NFL players resemble overgrown Bubble Boys, isolated and kept away as much as possible from their fans.

Ah, but there's another place you can reach them: when they are walking the runway.

If you plan to speak truth to authority, this is not a bad way to do it. The powerful czar heard the voices, no question, but his Praetorian Guard could not easily or quickly identify where they were coming from or who they belonged to. Besides, they had other things on their mind; they had to get their man safely into the building. It is harder to be spotted and identified when you heckle in a crowd and easier to slip away if someone does ID you. This is true for any situation.

BEST

There is safety in numbers, in heckling and in most other things as well. Not that Patriots fans felt threatened or in jeopardy in any way; rather, they just wanted to put a statement on the record at New England's 2015 home opener against the Pittsburgh Steelers. Traditionally the NFL commissioner appears at the home opener of the previous season's Super Bowl winner, which was New England, but on this night Goodell decided to take a pass, saying through a spokesman that he was going to watch the game on TV at home rather than come to Foxboro and cause a sideshow that would detract from football.

New England fans saw Goodell as an archvillain in Deflategate and would have surely brought down the house with boos if he had showed his face. Even with him not there, though, they got their point across in the fourth quarter when thousands of them started to chant, "Where is Roger? Where is Roger?" Each time they posed the question it grew in volume and intensity. Listening to the crowd, Cris Collinsworth, the ex-NFL receiver working the game from the TV broadcast booth, said, "I gotta say I agree with them."

When you speak truth to power and you have the numbers behind you, it's no longer heckling. It's called democracy.

The runway is that short strip that leads into and out of the interior of the stadium where the locker rooms are. Players walk the runway before and after every game, and at the end of the first half when they go into the locker room and then when they reemerge to play the second half.

The runway is uncovered, and you can get unusually close to the players. Closer than you get when you're in an end zone section—unless, of course, a player does a Lambeau Leap into your lap—or the 50-yard line or anywhere else. And they are walking, not running. Many of them have their helmets off and you can see their faces. The game has stopped, they are tired, their defenses are momentarily down. Granted, this window of opportunity does not last long, but it is there, and when it opens you can speak directly to them, without filters, and deliver a positive, uplifting message in support of your boys.

Or *not*.

New York Jets fans, suffering under the last years of Rex Ryan's reign as head coach, chose to take the latter tack in a 2012 game at the Meadowlands in which the club was, all too typically, being hammered. As the beleaguered Jets players—resembling the cast of *Les Misérables*—walked forlornly off the field, down the runway, and into the locker room, their unhappy fans let loose on them:

Heckler #1: "You're pathetic. You are pathetic. You suck. You're pathetic, every one of you. You suck."

Heckler #2: "Unf**kingbelievable! You guys are a disgrace."

Heckler #3: "You suck! Bums!"

Heckler #4: "You're terrible. Garbage. Garbage. Garbage."

This last heckler was jabbing his finger at various players as they walked past him, making sure each of them got the message that he was garbage, garbage, garbage. The hecklers stood above the players in the seats, leaning over the railing and screaming down at them. It was easy to envision a fan throwing something or pouring a cup of beer over a player's head, although none did. Apart from this, little restraint

Rex Ryan and his Jets got slammed on the runway.

was shown, as these fans were too pissed and they cared too much. Their anger and sense of betrayal over how the Jets—*their team*—were playing was real and profound. *You let us down, and now we're going to make you pay.*

This venting took place at the end of the first half; there was still another half to go. One can only imagine what the scene was like after the fourth quarter. Although with YouTube you do not need to use your imagination. Cue up another video and another Jets loss, this time to their bitter rivals, the Patriots coached by Bill Belichick. New England had won a Super Bowl and a half dozen AFC East titles while Ryan was coaching New York, and the Patriots were pounding the Jets yet again as the first half ended in a game at the Meadowlands. As the Jets walked the runway, a heckler spotted Ryan amongst them and shouted, "Hey Rex, Belichick is better than you."

Ryan, no shrinking violet, wasn't having any of it. He looked up and said, "Shut the f**k up." The heckler laughed in triumph because he had planted his stinger and pierced the bubble.

CHAPTER 7

How to heckle: The 20 essential rules of heckling

If, after the New York Jets had reached the quiet and safety of their locker room free for the moment from the venomous anger of their fans, someone had asked then-head coach Rex Ryan and his squad about the right of hecklers to freely speak their minds, they surely would not have responded with a passionate defense of the First Amendment. More probably they would have cited the Second Amendment and talked about how they were going to get a gun and—well, not *kill* one of those fans. Just maybe wound him in the leg so they could—to borrow a line from Johnny Cash—watch him bleed.

Actually, some of the Jets players and coaching staff may have agreed with the fans. Some may have thought, "Yeah, it sucks being yelled at like that. But you know what?

They're right. We stink." In this way the heckling minority gives voice to what the majority thinks, although most fans prefer not to express their unhappiness so directly or using such harsh language. They prefer to join thousands of others in the stadium in a ringing chorus of boos. Frequently team owners and management gain popularity by taking the side of unhappy fans and criticizing their own players. This criticism is also a form of heckling, although because billionaire owners and their employees are the ones doing it, nobody calls it that.

North of Vancouver on Whistler Mountain, one of the sites of the 2010 Winter Olympics, organizers of a summer mountain biking festival have come up with an ingenious solution for what to do with hecklers. It's called "Heckler's Rock," and it's a popular feature of the Canadian Open off-road bicycle race that is held at the festival, which attracts tens of thousands of enthusiastic college-age cyclists (and partiers) every year. Bike riders race over the mountain course and pass by Heckler's Rock, where, as one man said, "heckling is the name of the game and no one is spared." Hecklers blow horns, ring bells, make constant noise, chant, curse, and cheer, all the while drinking and smoking to frat party excess. Some of the girls lift their tops and expose their breasts a la Mardi Gras. One youthful celebrant explained the appeal of the place: "We get drunk, naked, and get some photos. You can do all three at once at Heckler's Rock."

As instructive as this example is, it is doubtful that the NFL or any other pro sports league or team would reserve a section in their stadiums for hecklers only, granting them carte blanche to drink, get high, get naked, crowd surf, and cavort like maniacs. Probably would be a popular section, though, not unlike the Raiders' unofficial Black Hole.

One reason this will never happen is that hecklers arguably have no real power; they are seen basically as just guys in the peanut gallery, bleacher bums. They can be easily dismissed, ridiculed, and marginalized by those who have official power in sports, and by those in the media and elsewhere who wish to brownnose those in power. Hecklers do not just interrupt the games and annoy the players; they sometimes interfere with the business of sports too. And lots of people and concerns— athletes, companies, advertisers, media, TV networks, arenas, ballparks, stadiums, teams, leagues—do not like this, often for understandable and justifiable reasons. They wish hecklers would simply mind their own business.

Nevertheless, hecklers are not going away. They are above all fans with a deep personal connection and loyalty to their teams. They have an urgent desire and need to express themselves, and this will never change. While recognizing the pressures against them, they—you, we—need to be smart, stay smart, and observe the 20 fundamental rules of the art of heckling.

1. Stay in the game.
The first rule of heckling is the first rule of life: Survive. It makes no sense to get tossed from the game for saying or doing something in clear violation of the arena's or team's fan code of conduct. You're there to make a difference, right? You're there to help your team. The only way you can do this is by sticking around.

If you're unclear about the rules, review your team's website regarding fan behavior. Warnings and guidelines are also found on the backs of tickets and season ticket applications. But all these rules are subject to local interpretation and enforcement, which brings us to Fundamental No. 2.

2. Evaluate your environment and the people in it.

Wherever you sit, you will inevitably take a look around at the ushers and stadium personnel in your area. They are just ordinary working stiffs, men and women who want to do their jobs and enjoy the game with no problems. Whether they escort you to your seat or serve as stadium security or are selling programs, they deserve your respect and cooperation.

Know where your
stadium usher is!

That being said, it will most likely be an usher who issues you a first warning and tears your ticket. If there is a second offense, a torn ticket tells security that you have had a previous warning. A second offense may get you tossed. But you may not receive two warnings in every case. You can get ejected on a first offense, depending on the violation and the person responsible for enforcing it.

What bothers one usher may not bother another. You can rag on a visiting player and sometimes the usher will enjoy it, sympathize with it, and kindly ignore it. But ushers will respond to complaints from other fans, especially parents with children. So you need to be aware of who else is sitting in your area.

3. Do not enter the no-fly zones.

Hecklers can be warned or thrown out of a game for the most seemingly banal offenses. One fan told the story of watching a game in Yankee Stadium in which a New York patron heckled Baltimore Orioles outfielder Nick Markakis, distorting his name by calling him "kay-kiss." This brought security personnel, who demanded to see the heckler's ticket. When he refused they escorted him from the park.

But most hecklers understand the no-fly zones, the acts that will get them immediately tossed:

- Cursing heavily, particularly around children.

- Using racial or ethnic slurs or engaging in Dr. Dre–like misogynist patter.

- Obvious acts of drunken imbecility, such as running onto the field naked.

Stay off the field and keep your clothes on. Nor is it good form to make like some English Premier League soccer hooligan and try to fight the bloke next to you whose only crime against humanity is that he happens to be wearing the other team's gear. Do any of these things and security will likely come crashing down upon you.

4. Bring a wingman. Or wingwoman.

Earlier in the book we told the story of a Pittsburgh heckler who got all over Ryan Braun—"Hey Braunnnnnn . . ."—at PNC Park. At one point the heckler yelled at the Milwaukee outfielder to "stop playing with your junk out there," a comment that elicited a hasty warning from his girlfriend, who was filming him. She told him to watch his language and he replied, "No, I'm allowed to say 'junk.' It's allowed."

This is a useful anecdote for two reasons: First, it shows that the heckler is aware of the no-fly zones at PNC and wants to stay clear of them; and second, it points out the value of a wingman or wingwoman, who plays a variety of useful roles.

She is likewise leery of those no-fly zones and may wish to stay even farther away from them than you. Equally important: She laughs at your jokes. As any comedian will testify, it is tough to play a house where people aren't laughing at your jokes. Your wingwoman can act as ambassador too, creating goodwill among those who are sitting nearby as well as any ushers in the area. Another valuable role she plays is to film your pearls of wisdom and upload them for friends and followers to see online.

5. Lighten up and have some fun.

This is not to say lighten up in your heckling of the opposition, if you are so moved. Rather, it means lighten up in *your attitude* about heckling. There's a difference.

At a game at Madison Square Garden, Spike Lee was heckling Cleveland Cavaliers point guard Mark Price, who was pretty much pointless in the first half, as Lee reminded him when he was warming up before the start of the third period. "Mark Price," said Lee, reading loudly from the stat sheet so Price could hear him. "Two for ten, five turnovers. Hey Mark, do we have a chill tonight? Coming down with something?"

Price smiled and responded the best way a player can, by sinking a bunch of Reggie Milleresque shots in a row. After one bucket he ran past Lee and playfully pulled his Knicks cap down over his eyes. Now it is almost certain that no player you are heckling will ever want to pull your cap down in the spirit of bonhomie, but you get the idea.

6. Have a drink.

Some people dis hecklers because many of them drink. What's the problem? A beer baron founded one of baseball's greatest franchises, the St. Louis Cardinals, and Anheuser-Busch owned it for many years; the ballpark where the Cardinals play still bears its name. The beer industry brought energy, jobs, and a sense of identity to the city of Milwaukee, whose baseball club pays tribute to this history in its name, the Brewers. Every professional sports park and arena sells beer and wine, and beer and alcohol advertising and sponsorships play a vital economic role in sports and have done so for well over a century. Beer and ball go together like beer and heckling.

7. Do your research.

This is standard advice for hecklers, but it bears repeating because research will keep your material fresh and entertaining, not boring and repetitive. If you know nothing specific about the guy you are heckling, the tendency will be to fall back on trite and tired heckling clichés. With Wikipedia, research today is so easy there's almost no excuse not to do it. Riff on what you see there, making fun of a guy's minor league background, where he's from, whatever. Maybe just read his bio aloud. That works too.

The best hecklers, like the best comedians, are topical and edgy. Knowing the latest on a player will keep you on trend.

8. Be spontaneous.

Research is only good up to a point, though. Be spontaneous. For example, you may be heckling some guy and learn that for the past three innings you have been calling him by the wrong name. Oops. That's laughable to the player and makes you look foolish. On the other hand, once you find out the truth, instead of switching to the right name keep calling him by the wrong one, over and over. It becomes a shtick that may irritate the player and make people laugh.

Another virtue of spontaneity is that things come out of nowhere and sometimes they're funny. One example of this was a game in Chicago between the hometown White Sox and the Cleveland Indians, with Grady Sizemore of the Tribe up at bat. It was the 11th inning, very late at night, and the few fans who had stuck around to see the end of the game were anxious to move things along. Not so Sizemore who, in the spirit of Mike Hargrove—nicknamed "the Human Rain Delay" for the interminable amount of time he spent getting ready in the batter's box before each pitch—did not seem to care what time it was, or how long it took him to bat.

After taking a pitch for ball one, he stepped out of the box and stared blankly down at the third-base coach. He stood

Let slow batters know someone's in labor. Hurry up!

there looking almost catatonic although he was the guy holding the bat in his hands. At long last he stepped back into the box apparently ready to hit, and this was when a White Sox heckler yelled out, his voice clear and loud as a ringing bell, "Hey Sizemore, my sister told me she's pregnant. Come on, you jerk!"

The comment was so unexpected that the TV broadcasters calling the game laughed out loud on the air, and even went so far as to speculate as to what the heckler meant by his remark. They decided that his pregnant sister could be in labor, and that Sizemore needed to hurry up before she gave birth. Or something. Of course, the heckler may not have a sister at all. He may have just made it up. You know, a joke.

9. Use props.

All the great hecklers use props, including the great movie hecklers.

Take Robert Downey Jr. Actually, to call him a great movie heckler is a bit of a reach, although he is a great movie actor. In one of his earliest film roles he played a goofball character in the Rodney Dangerfield comedy *Back to School*. Sitting in the stands, watching a diving competition, Downey turns to a friend and says, "You know what you almost never see? Somebody heckling a diver."

Wearing sunglasses and a hat, the future Iron Man and Sherlock Holmes shoots off a noisemaker just as a diver is dismounting from a high platform. The noise startles the diver, who flops into the pool. "You're all right, kid," the friend tells Downey, who, emboldened by his success, pulls a mirror out of his bag of tricks. This he uses to reflect the sunlight into

The "Distracted Diver."

the eyes of another diver on the platform, and the blinding glare produces another belly flop.

A noisemaker and a mirror? Surely you can do better than that.

10. Be unpredictable.

Not every heckle needs to be on the nose. "Stewart," one heckler shouted at outfielder Shannon Stewart, "your skills are inadequate!" The humor comes from the use of the word "inadequate," atypical for hecklers. Outfielder Scott Van Slyke has a beard big enough to hide a small rodent in it, prompting heckler Bobby Crosby to call out to him, "Hey Van Slyke, your beard is a commodity in Peru!"

What a beard has to do with the Peruvian commodities market is anyone's guess, but the absurd unpredictability of the line got laughs and that is all that counts. You don't have to dumb your heckling down just because some may not get the

Nonverbal heckling

With the PC police and the sports establishment curbing what you can say as a heckler, it may be time to consider nonverbal forms of communication. Here are some suggestions on how to get your message across without uttering a word.

Middle finger salute. The old reliable. A favorite not just of hecklers but of professional athletes too, who use it to express their opinion of what hecklers say to them.

Thumbs-down. This ancient expression of disapproval dates from Roman gladiator times and still has meaning today. Double your pleasure with a double thumbs-down.

Accusatory pointing. This is popular in basketball after a player commits a foul. Point your index finger at him and chant rhythmically, "You! You! You!"

Old reliable.

Finger foul count. Another technique is to count out the number of fouls a player has and show your fingers when you do: one, two, three, etc. This is best during March Madness when a player fouls out and you count him out with one hand. Yer outta here!

joke. On a Sunday afternoon game in Seattle, Jesus Montero looked terrible at the plate, prompting one heckler to tell him, "It's okay to work on the Sabbath, Jesus."

"I hope you know Japanese!" or "You better start learning Japanese!" are two taunts that you might hear at minor league parks, directed at struggling Triple-A or Double-A players who can no longer make the grade in the States and may need to go to Japan to earn a paycheck playing ball. The only problem with being too out-there in your references is that having to explain a joke is a sure sign it did not work in the first place.

Choke sign. Like the thumbs-down, the choke sign can be done with one hand or two. Place your hand or hands around the base of your throat to indicate that a player has swallowed something he cannot digest—that he is choking the game and is about to choke down a loss.

Crotch grab. The crotch grab carries a similar message as the choke sign but centers on another part of the human anatomy. Touch your crotch area with one or two hands to indicate to a player that he has no balls and lacks manhood.

Throat slash. This gesture—a slice of the hand or index finger across the base of the throat—expresses sharp contempt and disapproval.

Not just a way to ask for the Heimlich.

11. Ignore the haters.

One oft-heard criticism of hecklers is that since they never played sports at the highest levels, they have no business attacking those who do. (Of course, this same criticism could apply to many managers, coaches, front office executives, owners, and members of the media.) Best to just go about your business and remember the words of Randy Gill, aka "White Chocolate," a street ball shooting and dribbling legend who, while never ascending to the lofty heights of the NBA, played in college and in the minor basketball associations and understood his job as a player and entertainer far better than many brand-name superstars.

"I mean, I've been playing this game a long time, so you know that happens," he told a TV interviewer who asked him what it felt like to be heckled in a game. "If you are at a high level, you got to be willing to take criticism just like you take praise. So with me I know you guys [the hecklers] are very supportive of your team, the whole team, and great followers and fans of the game, so I got nothin' but love for y'all, y'know what I'm sayin'? You all can heckle me all day. You know with the popcorn popping we gonna put a show on. It's all good."

12. Take a cue from the master.

Nobody in show business has had a longer or better career insulting people than Don Rickles, who has heckled the likes of Frank Sinatra and Johnny Carson as well as the portly manager and coach Don Zimmer ("I've reserved three seats for you at my show tonight. One for you, one for your wife, and one for your stomach.") and slugger Reggie Jackson in his hair-growing prime ("Have you seen Reggie's afro? If his hair gets any longer, he'll need a ladder to put his hat on. If Reggie got a haircut, he'd be a midget."). The stars insulted by Rickles are generally charmed and flattered by his rudeness because they know it's an act, and off-stage he is evidently one of the world's nicest guys, a genuine sweetheart. (Born in the years before the Depression, he is still performing as of this writing, by the way.)

In an interview with the *Wall Street Journal*, Rickles explained the key to his success, beginning with his upbringing in the Jackson Heights section of Queens during the

Depression: "In school, I wasn't a wiseguy. I had the same attitude that I have on stage today. My personality is such that I'm never hurtful and I can get away with being a smart aleck. People just need to know up front that your intent isn't personal."

This is good advice for hecklers too, as are his words about being spontaneous and trusting yourself: "I never think about what I'm saying when I perform. I never say, 'Oh God, I shouldn't have said that.' In my business, if you worry about what you're saying, you fail."

13. Go old school. Or not.

Some heckles are as old as the giant redwoods, such as these two insults for umpires: "You couldn't make a call from a phone booth" and "Check your message machine when you get home because you've been missing calls all day."

Search Google for "great sports heckle lines" and you will find many more similar ones that deserve to be placed in a retirement home for old jokes. To a poor fielder: "Did you lose the instructions on how to use your glove?" "You can't even catch a cold!" After a lousy player hits a double: "That's the first time you've gotten to second base since your high school prom." There are the ones that mock a player's manhood, such as how he "sits when he pees." Or how he's a sissy if he lets a catchable fly ball drop in front of him in the outfield: "Way to get to the ball, Cinderella!" Or when a catcher makes a poor throw and a runner on first easily steals second: "Next time throw your purse at him."

Still, one person's old may be another's new. Although it has seen lots of use, this taunt to a bad hitter—"My blood alcohol level is higher than your batting average!"—may not be ready for mothballs yet. (Another tactic is to repeat the hitter's average to him when he comes up to bat.) After a catcher does something wrong, say: "You only have one job; figure it out!" Or to an old veteran: "Hey, let's cut you open and count the rings." Or to a bad ref: "Hey, the Jerk Store called. They're running out of you." All these old-school lines may draw reactions from people who have never heard them before.

Some heckling topics can be fresh in one era but eventually reach their expiration date, like steroids. Barry "Barroid" Bonds of the Giants heard heckling about his drug use whenever he journeyed outside San Francisco, as did Alex Rodriguez of the New York Yankees, especially when he traveled to Boston. Fans there chanted, "You take steroids [clap-clap-clap clap clap]. You take steroids [clap-clap-clap clap clap]." Although steroid heckling has, for now, lost some of its vigor, if there are any future PED revelations involving star athletes it will surely come back with a vengeance.

The best old-school heckles are timeless, such as when you yell to an outfielder, "Hey, your shoes are untied!" in the hopes of getting him to look down to check. This is a good one for kids. If the player actually takes the bait and looks down at his feet, it is a moment to be treasured.

14. Look for your opening and when it comes, strike!

Timing matters in heckling. Wait for a break in the action and make sure people can hear you. Don't be shy; give it what you got. Delivery matters too.

All this—timing, delivery, opportunity—came together for one San Francisco heckler when an aging Aaron Rowand, in the latter stages of his career, was manning centerfield for the

Giants. "I was at a Giants game in AT&T Park sitting in center field," the heckler recalled proudly in a Reddit post, years after the fact. "Aaron Rowand dogged it on a short fly ball that dropped in front of him. People were doing the 'Oh man, you suck' routine as the play was still going on, but when the play was

Timing matters in heckling.

over, a quiet lull set in on the crowd and Rowand started walking back towards us. I shouted, 'It's okay Aaron. We can't all be 30 again!' He looked directly at me, and I knew he heard."

15. "Baby" your target.

A heckler has numerous lines of attack. Old age, such as with Rowand, is one of them. A player's diminutive stature ("Hey where'd you get those pants, Baby Gap?") and slowness afoot ("Do you know why Benjie Molina wears No. 1? That's how many bases he reaches on a double.") are two more. Another classic is to insult his maturity and call him a baby.

Robin Ficker did this routinely. It was such a familiar tactic for him that when he made a return appearance at a Washington Wizards game—after staying away from the NBA for more than a decade—he employed it to keen effect and managed to get under the skin of Roy Hibbert of the Indiana Pacers. The Pacers were the visiting team that night at Verizon Center.

Ficker sat not far from the visitors' bench, and as he told a blogger, "I was talking to [Hibbert], telling him he looked very tired. He looked like my bicycle—'two tired'—and he needed a rest and needed to take a nap." Ficker said Hibbert should "take a hot bath with his favorite toy," and that he had brought his granddaughter's rubber ducky with him and that the 7-foot-2 Pacers center could take it and "relax like your mom would tell you and maybe take a nap."

Ficker may have been a little rusty after being away from heckling for so long, because Hibbert scored 15 points and grabbed seven rebounds, most of them coming in the second half, when Ficker was doing his baby routine. "He woke me up," said Hibbert. "He got me going and I let him hear it." Hibbert accused Ficker of yelling obscenities, which Ficker denied, saying he never used swear words. He said there was another heckler sitting near him and this may have been the person Hibbert heard. This fan did receive a warning for language.

"I was just trying to help the guy," Ficker said about the Pacers' big man. He argued that since Hibbert himself confessed that the heckling woke him up, what he said about him looking tired and being a big baby was spot-on. "Which confirms to me that he did look very tired and he did need a nap and he did need a hot bath with his rubber ducky toy," Ficker said.

16. Be adaptable.

A successful heckler entertains the fans around him. But some fans may not find you or your act entertaining. If someone asks you to stop, the best thing may be to take a break for a while. Or try a different approach than what you've been doing up to that point. Later in the game, if the irritated fan has gone home, you can go back to hurling daggers if that is more your style.

This is not to suggest you should take a nap and curl up with your rubber ducky at the first sign of resistance. Ficker did not, nor should you depending on the circumstance. At one college baseball game a raucous group of undergrads was getting on this one player, causing a girl who was sitting a few rows in front of them to turn around and inform them in an offended tone, "Hey, that's my brother you're yelling at." One of the hecklers instantly shot back, "Why are you telling me this? That's not something to be proud of."

We never learned how the story ended—whether the boys kept heckling the girl's brother—but they probably found someone else to pick on.

17. Play fair.

Hecklers sometimes offer to stop heckling in exchange for something from a player, such as a baseball. And players will sometimes comply to get hecklers off their back. Here are two examples of this, one good, one bad.

Mike Cameron of the Seattle Mariners made this offer to a heckler who was ragging on him: If he hit a home run on his next at bat, the fan had to leave the park. If Cameron didn't, he'd give the heckler a Mariners cap. Cameron did as he said—hit a home run—but the fan refused to leave his seat and continued to say outrageous things even after the outfielder socked a second home run. Bad show.

Good show: As Chicago White Sox pitcher Chris Sale was warming up in the bullpen prior to the start of a game in Detroit, Random Jerry, a regular fixture at Tigers home games, was ripping him: "Shouldn't you be at Walmart, Sale? That's a hideous beard but you're not going to make the playoffs anyway." The banter was just irksome enough to wreck the concentration of the ace lefty, who tossed Random Jerry a free ball to get him to shut up. Random Jerry happily took the ball and shut up, adding, "That's capitulation right there. He knew he didn't want to deal with me. I feel like a winner."

Heckling is a game within a game.

Heckling is a game within a game. Play fair. If you make a commitment with a player or someone else, follow through on it.

18. Be a hero.

Heckler as hero? That's a stretch for most people, including hecklers, but it may not be as farfetched as one might think. Consider this encounter some years ago on a Toronto street between a heckler and right fielder Alex Rios, then playing for the Blue Jays. This was after hours, in the evening, and Rios, dressed in a tux, was leaving a building after attending a charity dinner. It had been a bad day for the two-time All-Star; earlier he had gone hitless and struck out five times in a Blue Jays loss at Rogers Centre.

As he walked toward a limousine waiting for him on the street, a young boy approached him and asked him for his autograph. The ballplayer said no and brushed by the boy as if he wasn't there.

Watching all this was an anonymous man standing in the area with other onlookers. Reacting to Rios's rude treatment of the boy, he said, "The way you played today, Alex, you should be lucky somebody wants your autograph."

Sunglasses perched on his head although it was night-time, Rios turned sharply and snapped, "Who gives a f**k?

Who gives a f**k?" The man, wearing a Jays cap on his head turned around backward, apparently did. "You're a bum," he said. "You're a bum." Rios told him to "f**k off" and called him a "f**king idiot."

Making no effort to conceal his anger or disgust, Rios slid into the backseat of the limo. A security person approached the heckler and told him to move on. The heckler did as he was told but not before firing one last volley. "You forget where you come from, eh," he said to Rios.

In a CBC Sports account of the incident, the reporter cited Rios's ethnic background (he's from Puerto Rico) but said nothing about the boy, who was black. The heckler engaged Rios only after Rios blew the boy off and refused the autograph. He wasn't doing it for attention; his back is to the camera, and he was never identified. He was doing it to stick up for the boy.

Rios later apologized for his behavior. "I just lost my cool in that situation," he said. "You shouldn't act like that."

19. Give them their due.

Major league ballplayers like Alex Rios are not villains or heroes to be placed on pedestals and idolized. They're just like the rest of us, except for the amount of money in their bank accounts, the cars they drive, the mansions they live in, the rap stars and celebrities they hang with, the number of bikini-clad babes who attend their pool parties, and a few other trifling details.

Recognizing this about them—that they are just regular guys after all, regular guys who stand 6-foot-7 and weigh 350 pounds, who can palm a basketball like it's a tomato and do a windmill slam dunk, and who can turn on a 100 mph fastball and drive it 450 feet over the center field fence—it is important for hecklers to give them their due, when such a thing is truly warranted. One Reddit contributor told about going on a road trip with some of his buddies and watching the Cincinnati Reds play at Dodger Stadium in Los Angeles. "We had great seats behind the visitors' dugout," he recalled. "But one of my friends is kind of an a**hole. Joey Votto [Cincinnati first baseman] struck out his first three at bats and my friend gave him sh*t every time, as the on-deck circle was right in front of us."

But in his fourth at bat Votto turned the tables on the Dodgers and the heckler, cracking a three-run home run to give the Reds the lead. "On his way back to the dugout," said the fan, "he looked right at my friend and gave him a cool little finger gun shot and a wink. Made me a lifelong Votto fan." You gotta give it up for those guys when they deserve it—and they do, quite often.

20. Go to your go-to.

There is, of course, one never-fail, always reliable, go-to expression that every heckler can count on in a pinch. It is a drop-dead, fail-safe thing to say that is guaranteed to amuse, entertain, delight, offend, outrage, irritate, shock, horrify, electrify, excite, and stir condemnation as well as approbation.

What, you don't know this powerful expression? Oh, yes you do. Turn to the next chapter, and as Arsenio Hall always said, let's get busy with it.

CHAPTER 8

The incredible, inevitable, unavoidable "You suck!" chapter

One of the constants of language is change. Words and phrases become popular, appear everywhere, then drop off the planet as if they never existed at all. "As if." "Whatever." "Far out." If you still say "groovy" when you mean a thing is sick or rad or dope or the bomb—well, that's just grody to the max, dude. Gag me with a spoon, or as Vinnie Barbarino would have put it, "Up your nose with a rubber hose." Those who still text LOL or OMG—your time is coming too, if it hasn't already, because such abbreviations are so five minutes ago. Same with trolling, which is when someone talks trash online—uh no, talks smack . . . sorry, talks noise—well, whatever the latest term for dissing someone is. And if you're now trending you may have trended so much you are no longer on trend. Or something.

You will be pleased to know, however—or not so pleased, depending on your view of things—that one term remains impervious to the ever-changing nature of language. It is as current today as it was in Vinnie Barbarino's time. People are still trippin'—hippie phrase, fallen out of favor, now making a comeback with youth, soon to return to the slang graveyard—on it, especially in sports. When asked how a recent Oakland Raiders team was playing, All-Pro cornerback and wine connoisseur Charles Woodson used the term in question: "We suck," he said.

Draymond Green of the Golden State Warriors also called on the word during Oakland's victory parade after the Warriors beat the Cleveland Cavaliers to win the 2015 NBA title. A TV reporter asked the talented all-around forward—drunk with victory or perhaps high on life, let's just say he wasn't feeling any pain—for his opinion of the vanquished Cavaliers. He answered succinctly, "They suck."

His star teammate on the Warriors, shooting guard Klay Thompson, who was being interviewed on camera with Green, made a face and stepped back, as if to signal he wanted no part of what had just been said. Of course, his displeasure had nothing to do with Green's use of the word "suck," which Thompson no doubt freely uses himself, but rather the fact that his buddy had just handed the Cavs inspirational bulletin board material for the next time they faced the Ws.

"Suck" is popular in college ball too. In February 2014 the University of Iowa's Zach McCabe missed a potential game-tying shot with only seconds left in a close scrum against the University of Wisconsin. The Badgers went on to win and angry Iowa fans flooded Twitter with anti-McCabe tweets, blaming him for the loss. The unhappy forward tweeted his reply: "The fact that I have Iowa fans saying sh*t [to] me is insane. You fans suck. Suck a fat one all of you." He later deleted the post and said he was sorry—too late. Iowa head coach Fran McCaffery reacted by banning the use of Twitter by McCabe and every other Hawkeye player for the rest of the season.

Indiana University basketball coach Tom Crean got into hot water—outdated phrase; a more current way to put it is this: He stepped into a steaming pile of sh*t—when, after a tough loss to Wichita State during March Madness, he expressed his opinion about a referee in a way the referee would never misunderstand. "As the horn sounded," said a reporter who was there, "Tom Crean looked at official Kipp Kissinger across the floor and said, 'You suck.'" Many Indiana fans disapproved of this language and thought it inappropriate for a university official, although considering that Bob Knight once coached there, they should probably be grateful nobody threw any chairs.

The actor Emilio Estevez—you remember him, surely, for his triumph as Gordon Bombay, the coach in *The Mighty Ducks*—has merged fiction with real life by becoming an ardent fan of the Anaheim Ducks, whose team name derives from the film. After the Ducks beat the Chicago Blackhawks in an exciting overtime game in the NHL Western Conference finals, he was so thrilled he went all caps on Twitter: "SUCK IT, WINDY CITY WINDBAGS!!! DUCKS WIN! DUCKS WIN!" A bummer for Estevez, though: The Blackhawks outlasted the Ducks on the road to winning their third Stanley Cup in six years.

If we were to explore all the times that "suck" has been uttered in Estevez' terrain of Hollywood and pop culture, we would, as the phrase goes, be here all day. Only one need suffice—from *The Benchwarmers*, the David Spade–Rob Schneider masterwork in which a bully approaches a nerd on a baseball field and tells him to scram because he and his gang want to play there. "You suck," the bully tells him. "Don't you have a science test to study for?" But the nerd ultimately gets revenge after the bully gets knocked down in a fight and is lying helpless on the ground. The nerd rushes up and farts in his face.

A few years ago ESPN issued a memo to its broadcasters and commentators that said, in effect, that saying "suck" on the air sucked. Here is the memo:

> All,
>
> All of us in Production and throughout the company take great pride in the work of our on air talent. You are our direct connection with sports fans and contribute significantly in making ESPN the leader in sports media. Recently, there have been numerous incidents in which the word 'sucks' has been used on our air. This word is simply not appropriate for ESPN. What you say and the language you use is important for our audience and sports fans of all ages. Please be mindful of this starting immediately.

Signed by John Wildhack, executive vice president of production, and Laurie Orlando, senior vice president of talent development and planning, the memo did not, however, reach the desk of Charles Barkley at rival cable network TNT. Now a commentator for its *Inside the NBA* show, the great Hall of Fame star is known for his blunt candor and politically incorrect views, such as when he joked about the big bottoms of the women of San Antonio. "There's some big ol' women down here," he said during a broadcast of a San Antonio Spurs play-off game. "It's a gold mine for Weight Watchers." Adding, "Victoria is definitely a secret. They can't wear no Victoria's Secret down here."

The comments spawned outrage from San Antonio women who wore "Barkley Don't Know" T-shirts and chanted "Barkley sucks, Barkley sucks" in the background of a postgame *Inside the NBA* chat session at the Spurs' home arena. The chanting fans were down below in the seats while Barkley sat with his colleagues higher up in the arena. "I don't know if you can hear the San Antonio fans telling me I suck," he told viewers. "I just want them to know they suck too." He said this with good humor—the way he intended the fat jokes, he said—adding that most people in San Antonio recognized that he was just having fun. As for the grouchy grouches who can't take a joke, Charles restated his message for them: "I want them to know that I'm not just gonna take it. They suck too."

When Sir Charles, ESPN talent, the movies, Hollywood stars, and coaches and players in both the pro and college leagues freely employ the word—not to mention millions of others, young and old, across society—is it any wonder that hecklers do too? Given the sexual connotations of the term, it is a way to be nasty without being nasty, swearing without swearing. If you say "f**k" you're dead meat as a heckler. But "suck"? It's more of a gray area.

In a video survey of NBA players on heckling, correspondent Elie Seckbach asked Travis Outlaw of the Portland Trail-blazers what was the most common insult he heard from fans. The 6-foot-9 power forward looked at him with a world-weary

Rhymes with "itch," and other favorite baseball expressions

"There's no crying in baseball," Tom Hanks famously said in *A League of Their Own*. Maybe not. But there sure is a lot of swearing.

One of the all-time favorite swear words by players and the fans who heckle them is the one that rhymes with "itch." It suggests weakness or servility in one team and mastery by the opposing team, such as this student sign from a school that was about to play the University of Michigan in football: LET'S MAKE MICHIGAN OUR B*TCHIGAN.

TV baseball commentator Pedro Martinez, once a star pitcher for the Boston Red Sox, had troubles when he faced New York. Consequently hecklers in the Bronx crudely called him their "b*tch." Pedro brought still more ridicule onto himself when he told the media, "What can I say? I just tip my hat and call the Yankees my daddy." Every game after that Yankee fans would serenade him with chants of "Who's your daddy? Who's your daddy?"

Hecklers drop F-bombs all the time, an offense that can get them tossed. Same with "a**hole." "Balls," a slang word for two valuable parts of the male anatomy, can make for lighter amusement. After a shortstop fielded a grounder and bounced his throw to first, a heckler yelled, "Hey, this is baseball. If I wanted to see bouncing balls, I'd be watching *Magic Mike*." TV baseball analyst John Kruk was once a hard-hitting first baseman/outfielder for the Philadelphia Phillies. Diagnosed with testicular cancer, he underwent testicular surgery to stop the disease from spreading. Up at bat during a game, he took the first pitch and then stepped out of the box. "All right, John," said a heckler, "you got one ball now."

If hecklers would only clean up their acts, say some, they would be more entertaining and gain wider public acceptance. Tell that to Kevin Hart, Louis C. K., and other comedians who delight audiences by working blue. A joke that may not be funny when told clean can generate big laughs when peppered with some "f**ks" and "*itches." (Of course, there are no kids around when they perform, and their delivery and material are far superior to your average rowdy heckler.)

If you're a fan who is just trying to enjoy the game and some jerk near you insists on saying crude and disgusting things—which isn't heckling; It's just stupid—almost certainly you are not the only one who is unhappy. Tell the ushers and ask for him to be removed. If for some reason this cannot be done, ask to change seats or have your seats upgraded to a different section.

gaze and answered the only way he possibly could have. "You suck," he said. Seckbach—the first syllable of which is spelled with an *e*, by the way, not a *u*—concluded his report cheerily: "For the most part the players tell me they don't mind if people yell stuff at them, as long as it's original, entertaining, and in good taste."

"You suck" is not original or in good taste but it *is* entertaining, or can be, such as the time a Chicago heckler yelled out to a player, "You, in fact, suck!" Just that little spin—adding "in fact"—made it comical for the fans who heard it, similar to when another heckler shouted to a pitcher, "You suck," before adding in a more reasonable tone, "I just want you to know that."

You can tell a player that he sucks almost any time, in any sport, in virtually any situation. It is an all-purpose putdown and this may be partly why it has such an enduring hold on the sporting public. After Chase Utley of the Los Angeles Dodgers took out New York Mets shortstop Ruben Tejada and broke his leg with a hard slide at second base in a controversial play during the 2015 National League division series, Mets fans did not need to organize a convention to figure out what to say when the games shifted back to Citi Field and New York. "Utley sucks! Utley sucks!" they shouted before, during, and after the game. (New Yorkers also vented their anger with signs such as CHASE UTLEY LOVES ISIS and CHASE UGLY IS STILL PHILLTHY, a reference to Utley's days as an All-Star second baseman for the Philadelphia Phillies.)

The classic "You suck!" moment is naturally after a player screws up. Witness slugger Kris Bryant's much-heralded rookie debut with the Chicago Cubs in 2015. After a sterling prep and college career, the 23-year-old arrived in spring training looking like the reincarnation of Hack Wilson or Ernie Banks, bashing the ball all over the place. Cubs fans, desperate for somebody, anybody, to lift the club out of its traditional doldrums, crowded into Wrigley Field to see his major league debut, his first-ever game.

It did not turn out so hot for Bryant, who struck out his first three times at bat. After the third time he hung his head and walked dejectedly back to the dugout as Cubs fans, sharing his disappointment, sunk into silence. In the quiet of the ballpark a solitary voice could be distinctly heard: "You suck!"

As Chicago sportswriter Mike Oz noted, "Judgment comes swiftly in The 'Friendly' Confines." Still, Oz was not ready to pronounce a final verdict on the talented young Cubbie based on a single game: "One day isn't going to define Bryant's tenure with the Cubs, just like one fan yelling 'You suck' doesn't reflect what all Cubs fans think of their top prospect."

Time, and Bryant's performance, will ultimately determine what Cubs fans think of him, although we can say one thing with absolute certainty whether he ends up with a plaque in Cooperstown or gets sent back to Triple-A Iowa: He will hear "You suck" a million more times in his career. It may be as he heard it on the day of his debut—a simple but definitive "You suck!" Or it may be that fans attach his name to it, as in "You suck, Bryant!" Other variations will lead with his name: "Bryant, you suck!" or "Bryant sucks!" Whatever the exact usage, no one will doubt its meaning.

One "You suck" technique favored by hecklers is to read excerpts aloud from a player's Wikipedia page, starting by calling out his name. "Hey you [name of player], yeah, I'm talking about you." Then you start reading: "Born in Athens, Georgia. Weighs 215 pounds. Stands 6-foot, 1 inch tall. Bats right, throws left. Favorite movie: *Legally Blonde 2.*" Once you get the player's attention—and he will listen though he may pretend not to—you follow up with a sudden, definitive, "Yeah you, you suck!" This odd juxtaposition of elements—the ordinary facts of his bio culminating in "You suck!"—can cause laughter among nearby fans who also have been drawn into listening.

Spice up "You suck" with wiki-info.

One time a heckler was beating on Astros outfielder Carlos Lee, not using the Wikipedia gambit but just yelling "You suck" at him continuously for what seemed like hours. Finally Lee, who had just signed a $100 million contract to play for Houston, turned to the heckler and drew "1-0-0" with his finger in the air while mouthing the words "$100 million." Everyone in the bleachers got the joke and laughed, telling the heckler he had been bested and that he should sit down and shut up. It would be comforting to think that the chastened heckler did just that, but probably not.

Individual expressions of "You suck" have an undeniable power, to be sure, although the phrase becomes still more potent when a crowd of people gets in on the act. No one can ignore thousands upon thousands of fans, or possibly an entire stadium, saying it in unison. Chants of this nature are among the most powerful and powerfully disturbing in all of sports. Here are four of the greatest "You suck" moments in sports history.

Yale pranks Harvard: "We suck"

Students at our nation's institutions of higher learning frequently rely on "You suck" messaging. After the opening face-off college hockey student sections chant the name of the opposing goalie followed by a "You suck!" This is frequently combined with the traditional "It's all your fault! It's all your fault! It's all your fault!" or "Sieve! Sieve! Sieve!" after he lets in a goal.

Gary Glitter's "Rock 'n' Roll Part 2" is a favorite sports anthem, but due to Glitter's moral lapses University of Maryland administrators refused to let the school band play the song at a game. No matter. The student rooting section went ahead with it anyway, chanting "You suck!" and "We're gonna beat the hell out of you" on the beat without musical accompaniment.

Ohio State students got into a feud with ESPN commentator Mark May after May made critical remarks about its football team and cast doubts on its ability to keep up with powerhouse Arkansas in the 2011 Sugar Bowl. After OSU edged the Razorbacks in a thriller, Buckeye fans broke into chants of "Mark May sucks, Mark May sucks." The University of Florida student cheering section would chant "Move back, you suck! Move back, you suck!" each time the opposing team suffered a penalty in which it lost yards and had to move the line of scrimmage back. One older Florida graduate, deploring this new trend in student-led cheers, wrote on a *Gainesville Sun* message board, "I know I'm not the only one who thinks that cheering 'Move back, you suck' every time the opponent incurs a penalty is not a classy move. It may be cool or seemingly appropriate as an undergrad, but it reflects poorly on the rest of the fan base. Motion to make it stop." (The Gator band has since agreed to stop cueing the chant with a musical intro, and the chant has faded away.)

Criticizing these chants as inappropriate, while understandable, somewhat misses the point; the reason fans chant "You suck" is because it *is* inappropriate. And offensive. Not socially

What heckling is *not*

Some people confuse heckling, a legitimate fan activity, with illegitimate and illegal fan behavior. To dispel any confusion, here are three fan activities that are *not* heckling and not condoned. Doing any one of them will provide you with a uniformed escort off the field, out of the park, and perhaps to the local constabulary as well.

1. Running onto the field. Running onto the field will disrupt the game momentarily but likely not get you any camera time because TV generally does not show people doing this so as not to encourage potential copycats. The stupidest and funniest instance of a man running onto a field is shown at the start of every *Men in Blazers* program, when a drunken soccer fan sprints onto the pitch and nearly left foots a ball past the goalie. Good for giggles, as is the show.

2. Running onto the field naked. Streaking, as this is called, is the act of running onto the field of a sporting event or some other event without your boxers or anything else on. Guys—and streakers are mostly male; the ladies tend not to go for it as much—have done it at the Super Bowl, the Tour de France, Harvard-Yale football, and more.

3. Running onto the field to kiss a player. Streaking peaked as a fad in the 1970s, about the same time Morganna the Kissing Bandit was having her 15 minutes of fame. She garnered publicity for her regular job—nightclub stripper—by running onto the field during major league baseball games and trying to kiss stars like George Brett. Morganna had a 60-inch bosom. If you have her qualifications, give it a go. If not, stay in your seat and keep your pucker to yourself.

acceptable. An F-you to the other side without spelling it out. So it was in 2004 when Yale met Harvard in the final game of the football season between the two traditional Ivy League rivals. Harvard Stadium in Boston hosted the game that year, and welcoming Harvard supporters as they took their seats were members of the Harvard Pep Squad, a student cheer-leading group. Some carried megaphones to lead cheers and a few had their faces painted crimson and white. All handed out poster boards or large cards made of construction paper for a card routine to be performed by fans during the game.

There were 1,800 of these red and white cards, and the Harvard students, faculty, and alumni filing into the section thought what the Pep Squad was doing was fantastic. When the rally group gave the signal, everyone would flip the cards over to spell out the words "Go Harvard." Take that, Yalies.

But when they got the signal and flipped the cards over, just before the end of the first half, the words spelled out something else: WE SUCK.

The giant block letters were clearly visible to Yale's support-ers on the opposite side of the field, a number of whom glee-fully chanted, "You suck, you suck." The red cards formed the letters, the white cards the background. The Yale students who thought up the prank—the Pep Squad was a fiction, and its two dozen members were all in on the joke—could not believe it had actually worked.

It took some time before Harvard fans realized what they were doing, as only fans on the Yale side could fully see the message. (You can see it at a website devoted to preserving the memory of the moment, HarvardSucks.org.) So when the Pep Squad issued a second signal to flip the cards over, the

Go Harvard? Wrong. Harvard sucks.

fans obediently did as they were told and spelled it out again. Apparently this occurred several more times. Each time it did the jubilant fans on the Yale side followed with more "You suck" and "Harvard sucks" chants.

MLS adds a new wrinkle: YSA

Major League Soccer fans created a new twist on the classic "You suck!" formulation by attaching "a**hole" to the end. The chant is known by its acronym, YSA.

The "a**hole" being referred to changes depending on the team you are playing, but it is always the same guy: the other team's goalie. Here's how it works: The goalie has the ball and is about to make a goal kick. Both teams have moved back toward the middle of the field because typically the ball sails a long way after he puts his foot to it. The goalie usually takes some time before he makes his kick, setting the ball on the edge of the penalty box. As he steps back fans begin saying "Ohhhhhhh . . ." steadily building in intensity and volume.

Then, as the goalie rushes forward to make the kick, the crowd says loudly, all together, but just once: "You suck, a**hole!"

It's not clear how or when YSA began. Andrew Keh of the *New York Times* looked into the matter and described it as "a more vulgar expression of 'You suck, jerk.'" He said its origins may be in Latin America or Europe, where the fans tend to be rougher and more violently partisan than their American counterparts. Nevertheless, he concluded, YSA appears to be a product of Yankee ingenuity, "suggesting that early MLS fans . . . adopted the structure and added their own choice words."

MLS fans from Seattle to New York have chanted YSA at their games, and it has even been heard at U.S. men's national team games. The league's outraged head office sent letters to teams urging them to get their fans to stop saying it. "Members of Real Salt Lake Supporter Clubs," the MLS wrote to its Salt Lake City franchise, "are expected to demonstrate a universal commitment to eradicate YSA, its derivatives and other chants employing mass use of foul language, both at Rio Tinto Stadium [its home field] and on the road." League president Don Garber said it was "just infuriating to me. It's just so uncreative and ridiculous, and we need to stop it. Our broadcast partners don't like it. When vulgarity is going over the air, it's an issue with the FCC and we've got to stop it."

The MLS used a carrot-and-stick approach to combat YSA. If teams did not find ways to stop it they could be sanctioned, and fan groups would be prevented from displaying signs and banging on drums. At the same time the MLS offered to pay $500 per game—up to $2,000 total for four consecutive games—to fan groups that actively worked to suppress the chant and successfully did so.

The strategy seems to have worked, as the chant is less popular than it once was, although not because soccer fans have suddenly been beset by an attack of good manners. "It was a way to be antagonistic in a tongue-in-cheek way," Dave Hoyt of the Portland Timbers' fan group said about YSA. "It gets people's attention." His group doesn't say the chant anymore, only because it had been done so much that people were tired of it. "We still have plenty of chants that have blue language," he said reassuringly.

Potvin sucks, and so do the Rangers

On February 25, 1979, in a regular-season game at Madison Square Garden, Ulf Nilsson of the New York Rangers gathered up a puck on the Rangers' end of the ice as Denis Potvin of the New York Islanders skated toward him. What happened next continues to be debated decades later. Potvin, known for his rough, bare knuckles style of play—"one of the meanest hockey players who ever played," in the words of broadcaster Don Cherry—lowered his left shoulder and delivered a body shot to Nilsson, knocking him hard into the boards. The collision sent the Rangers center down onto the ice, broke his ankle, and prematurely ended his season.

The Montreal Canadiens beat the Rangers in the Stanley Cup finals that year, and bitter Rangers fans blamed Potvin for the loss. His hit was dirty, they said. If the talented Swede had been able to suit up for the series against Montreal, the Rangers might have won it all. It was Potvin's fault. Potvin was to blame.

For his part Nilsson never accused Potvin, who is now a broadcaster, of making an illegal hit. He said his ankle fracture was due to his skate getting caught in a small opening between the ice and the boards. Even so, it is generally agreed that Nilsson was never the same quality player he was before the injury, and as broadcaster Al Trautwig has said, "Rangers fans never forgot that hit, and the chants derisive of Denis Potvin exist to this day."

Indeed they do. All these years later, at Ranger home games at the Garden, fans do "Potvin sucks" chants, even though many of the younger ones have no knowledge of the inciting incident and no idea why they're chanting his name. Some may not know who Potvin is. And fans do it whether the Rangers are playing the Islanders, Devils, Mighty Ducks, or Sharks. It doesn't matter who the visitors are; they just like doing it. It's fun. It's tradition.

Sportswriter Flip Bondy says there is "a real art to the chant," which always begins with a series of whistles. Anyone can do the whistles, although they must be loud enough to be heard by fans sitting in sections away from the whistler. Put your index and pinky fingers in your mouth in the classic manner and give it a blow. The whistles have a rhythmic cadence, as if they are a mating call for the avian species *Rangerus newyork us*. One set we heard consisted of 15 whistles, short, medium, and long, culminating in three staccato bursts, after which the crowd, having grown quiet as it tuned into the message being delivered, shouted as one, "Potvin sucks!"

The best-known "Potvin sucks" whistler is Vinny Bova, a longtime Rangers fan who has been doing it for more than 20 years. At a game fans who spot him in his seat call out to him, "Hey Vinny, gimme a whistle." Vinny is usually happy to oblige, waiting until there is a lull in the action or a quiet moment in the arena before letting loose with his five distinctive shrieking whistles. "If we're losing by a lot, I'll do it," he told Bondy. "If we're winning by a lot, I'll do it. It's been going on for a long time, and some people don't like it but I think it's hilarious."

One of the people who didn't like it was his father, who would not let him say the word "suck" when they were going to games together years ago at the Garden. Now Bova has grown up and thinks "it's all in good fun. And it obviously gets on [Potvin's] and all the Islanders fans' nerves, which is an added plus."

One of the people who didn't like it was his father.

Islanders fans return the favor on their home ice when the organist breaks into a rendition of the "Chicken Dance" children's song. In the original, chicken-like clucking sounds are heard at various intervals. But instead of clucking Islanders fans joyfully sing out, "The Rangers suck." This gets repeated several times.

Fans of the New Jersey Devils also make use of a children's song to mock the Rangers. They rewrite "If you're happy and you know it, clap your hands," to say instead, "If you know the Rangers suck, clap your hands [clap, clap, clap]. If you know the Rangers suck, clap your hands [clap, clap, clap]. If you know the Rangers suck, and you know the Rangers suck," etc. Devils fans also have their version of the "Potvin sucks" chant, beginning with a similar set of whistling signals. But it is not Potvin who sucks, it is the Rangers.

Parenthetically, "Rock 'n' Roll Part 2" is also the unofficial fight song of the Devils and it is played over their arena's sound system after big moments. Team management disapproves of it, however, and has tried from time to time to replace it with a different song. But fans remain loyal to the Glitter tune. Each time it goes "Hey!" they chime in with a resounding "You suck!"

"Steinbrenner sucks! Steinbrenner sucks!"

In the annals of "You suck" sports history, no two teams can compete with the New York Yankees and Boston Red Sox. Their baseball rivalry even bleeds over into football.

After winning their first Super Bowl, in 2002, the New England Patriots held a parade in downtown Boston that attracted hundreds of thousands of Patriots fans, many of whom are also fans of the Red Sox. One Patriots player, reserve linebacker Larry Izzo, stood on the celebration stage at City Hall, held the Lombardi Trophy above his head, and shouted into the mic, "The Yankees suck!" This began a crowd chant of "The Yankees suck, the Yankees suck" that left veteran *Boston Globe* sportswriter Dan Shaughnessy shaking his head. "I guarantee you," he wrote, "if the New York Giants win the Super Bowl, nobody's going to start a 'Boston sucks' chant."

But Shaughnessy may have misjudged New York's sports fans, or forgotten what long memories they have. After the Giants beat the Patriots six years later in the Super Bowl, New York City held a ticker tape parade down Broadway that culminated with speeches at City Hall and a rousing crowd rendition of "Boston sucks! Boston sucks!"

Yankees who travel to Fenway Park routinely hear how badly they suck, and Red Sox who come to Yankee Stadium get the same treatment. Nobody will likely ever match the record of "You suck"s heard by Roger Clemens, a star pitcher for both teams at different stages of his career. Yankee and Red Sox fans have both let him know how much he sucks.

Because of their long record of success, their arrogant image, the money they spend to acquire free agents, and other reasons, the Yankees have surely heard more hecklers tell them they suck than any other franchise in sports. "Yankees suck" may be the most popular negative crowd chant ever. The Seattle Mariners issued a dictum to their fans a few years ago prohibiting them from bringing signs to the park saying "Yankees suck" or wearing T-shirts with this message. If fans failed to comply, ushers or security would confiscate the signs and ask for the T-shirts to be turned inside out. This rule ticked off one Seattle blogger, who expressed the sentiments of many: "Insulting the opposing team is almost as much fun as cheering for your favorite team, especially when the opponent is the New York Yankees."

The Onion, a satirical newspaper, joked that "Yankees suck" had become such a part of the American idiom that the team

Some "suck" chants are transcendent.

trademarked the phrase and now earns billions from its use. "U.S. Patent and Trademark Office records show that every time an individual chants, shouts, or writes the words 'Yankees suck,' the New York Yankees organization earns at least $2.15, an amount that escalates depending on repetition, volume, and whether the phrase was used during a national broadcast," it said. *The Onion* went on to say that the Yankees are making so much money from the phrase that they have acquired the rights to other popular anti-Yankee epithets such as "Jeter blows," "A-Roid," "A-Fraud," and "Jeter sucks, A-Rod swallows."

Ironically, the most notorious expression of this "marginally profane" chant—to borrow Flip Bondy's definition—was done by Yankee fans, in Yankee Stadium, and directed at one of the most powerful Yankees ever, team owner George Steinbrenner. The date was April 27, 1982, and the occasion was the return of Reggie Jackson to New York, but not under happy circumstances for Yankee fans. Jackson, whose home run-hitting heroics had led the team to back-to-back world championships in the 1970s, had left for California earlier in the year, signing with the then-California Angels as a free agent. Yankee fans faulted Steinbrenner for not pulling out the checkbook as he had done so many times in the past and stubbornly refusing to re-sign the popular if aging star.

This was Jackson's first game in Yankee Stadium in an Angels uniform. In the fifth inning, facing his old teammate Ron Guidry, he hit a single and scored the run that put the Angels ahead, 3–2. This was the score when Reggie came up in the seventh to face Guidry one more time. Guidry hung a slider and Jackson, who never let a big moment slip through his grasp if he could help it, sent it deep into the right field stands for a home run. The ball was hit so hard it thudded against the upper-deck facing and bounced back onto the field. As Jackson rounded the bases in triumph, Yankee fans chanted "Reg-gie! Reg-gie!" much as they had when he hit those three glorious home runs in the deciding game of the 1977 World Series.

Then things took a more ominous turn. Pissed-off fans pointed up at the owner's box on the mezzanine level, where

Steinbrenner was sitting, and began to chant, "Steinbrenner sucks! Steinbrenner sucks!"

There were 35,458 fans in the stadium that night, and although many had gone home earlier due to rainy weather, the ones who stuck around were making it clear how they felt, shouting repeatedly in unison, "Steinbrenner sucks! Steinbrenner sucks!"

This was surely not the first time a crowd of fans had used the word "suck" in a chant at a baseball game or another sporting event. But because of the extraordinary circumstances of the moment—the Yankees being the Yankees, Reggie being Reggie, George being George, all of this unfolding in the House That Ruth Built in the media capital of the world—this may have been when "You suck" entered the sports lexicon in a big way. From this point on the expression spread and became the commonplace that it is today.

But there was a personal impact too, not just historical. Yankee Stadium that night put a lie to the nursery rhyme about how sticks and stones will break my bones but words can never hurt me. Words hurt. Words sting. They cause pain. George Steinbrenner said it was one of the most humiliating moments of his life.

CHAPTER 9

Group dynamics:
How to turn one into many

Up in his owner's box, listening to the derisive chants of thousands of fans, George Steinbrenner felt, in the words of a biographer, "devastated." In a postgame meeting with the Yankee manager and coaches, he said he felt betrayed. "I can't believe what went on out there tonight," he said. "How could they do this to me? How could these fans, who I've done so much for, turn on me like this?"

One of the Yankee coaches, Jeff Torborg, could not hide his amusement, which made the owner react with anger mixed with self-pity. "What are you laughing about? You think this is fun? How would you like it if 40,000 people were yelling 'Torborg sucks, Torborg sucks?'" For this Torborg had no answer because he was not a big enough personality, only a bit player on the Yankee stage dominated by the giant figure of its owner. Only a rare unlucky few hear themselves mocked by a stadium of ticked-off baseball fans, and Steinbrenner was one of them. It was hardly the first time though. Fans had chanted "No more George! No more George!" before that night and would continue to do so periodically until the mid-1990s, when the Derek Jeter–Mariano Rivera era began and the Yankees' fortunes revived.

A 1990 *Newsweek* magazine cover story declared Steinbrenner "the most hated man in baseball." The haters included Yankee fans who felt that his frequent hiring and firing of managers, his chronic meddling in the decisions being made on the field, his constant criticism of players, and his lack of patience with young talent had hurt the team. By 2010, when Steinbrenner died and after the Yankees had added several more pieces of championship hardware to their well-stocked World Series trophy room, his reputation had been rehabilitated. He was now revered for his toughness, for his all-out commitment to winning, and for restoring the franchise to glory, most spectacularly the building of the new Yankee Stadium. "The House That George Built" was how an ESPN *30 for 30* documentary labeled it.

"Over the years the fans have changed their opinion of Steinbrenner," said Phil Pepe, a New York sportswriter who covered him all those years. "They started out liking him, and then the team started losing again and they didn't like him. Then they liked him again when they started winning again."

So it is with fans. So it is with hecklers. They will cheer you when you're up and they will kick you when you are down. The boss of the Yankees understood this. He got kicked but he did plenty of kicking too.

What characterized the "Steinbrenner sucks" chant was its spontaneity. Although many of the fans at Yankee Stadium that night came prepared to cheer their old hero Reggie and possibly boo their nemesis George, none of this would have occurred if Jackson had struck out in the seventh. His fans would have had nothing to cheer about and the Yankees owner could have sat undisturbed in his box, content in the wisdom of his decision to let the old slugger go west.

Reggie's blast launched the chant and it spread across the park. But how? Did it start with one lone wolf or a pack of them restlessly agitating from the same section? Or did two different sections, in different parts of the park, spontaneously start saying it at the same time, ultimately merging their efforts and leading others to join in? The dynamics of it are fascinating to contemplate, especially for hecklers. How does one become many? How do you go from one howling wolf to a whole pack of them all howling the same thing at the same time?

There are seven key elements to successful crowd chants. Although it is admittedly a tortured description, one might even call them "the seven characteristics of highly effective crowd heckling." They are a passionate core, shared knowledge, willingness to dare, tradition, seizing the opportunity, a catchy hook, and an Us against Them attitude. Let's consider them one at a time.

1. A passionate core

Whether a chant is spontaneous or the product of careful plotting matters less than the passion of the core participants. Their passion is everything.

Lots of sports fans love their team when it is winning. Then when it goes into a funk, not so much. The passionate core, in contrast, is indefatigable. They beat on drums, wear costumes, paint their faces, jump up and down, wave flags, post banners, arrive early, stay late, clap, hoot, drink copiously, and cheer lustily. In college sports the passionate ones can always be found in the same place: the student rooting sections. In soccer they often sit in special sections near a goal. Same with American football—down by the end zone. In major league baseball, in the bleachers. These are the cheap seats—"cheap" being a relative term, given how pricey pro sports have become—and the more casual, less passionate fans tend to congregate elsewhere. Which suits the core supporters just fine. They like the idea of being together and regard it as a badge of honor.

2. Shared knowledge

Charged by emotion and their unyielding loyalty, the passionate core leads the way; wherever they are, that is where chants are born. And if a "Sieve! Sieve! Sieve!" does not begin with them, once the core gets involved they will help spread the chant across the arena.

Yelling out "Sieve!" to a goalie is a standard (and, some would say, overused) ice hockey taunt, which you may not know if you do not follow the sport. This brings up the second characteristic of effective group heckling: shared knowledge. Team loyalty is a given, and passion, vital as it is, is not enough. You have to know things about the opposition in order to undermine it, and in this regard no one is better prepared and brings more knowledge to the table than college cheering sections.

Keep him chugging. If he stops, yell "Booooo!"

It is routine practice for students to pass out instructional sheets on how to harass visiting teams, spelling out what to yell and when to yell it, and providing detailed scouting reports on opposing players. "Heckling the goaltender is extremely important," said one cheat sheet distributed by and to Michigan State students. "If the goaltender begins to drink from his water bottle, repeatedly chant 'Chug!' Once the goaltender stops, shout 'Boo!' An example of this would sound like: 'Chug! Chug! Chug! Chug! Boooooooooo!'"

These instructions helpfully explain that "a sieve is the most derogatory thing you can call an opposing goaltender without resorting to profanity." (A sieve has holes and lets things through it, which a goalie should never do.) Not as derogatory perhaps, but still a major pwning, is to ridicule the goalie's looks. "If the goaltender takes off his mask," the Spartan sheet goes on, "repeatedly chant, 'Ug-ly goalie! [clap-clap-clap clap clap] until the goaltender puts his mask back on. An example of this would sound like: 'Ug-ly goalie! [clap-clap-clap clap clap] Ug-ly goalie! [clap-clap-clap clap clap].'" Worst of all is the u-g-l-y chant, which double-slams the goalie as an ugly sieve.

When the opposing team's starting lineup is introduced, as each player's name is announced and he skates onto the ice, the notes remind students to respond with a "Who cares? You suck!"

Students at one Southeastern Conference school prefaced their heckling CliffsNotes with the admonition that everyone should "try to be creative and disruptive but please refrain from foul language." Their "Heckling Help" sheet still contained enough dirt on a visiting basketball team to make a political opposition researcher proud. One player, said the notes, was "arrested last summer for driving 48 mph in a 10 mph zone without a license." Another has a nickname of Snoop and "he has no clue why." Another "enjoys taking shirtless pictures with his teammates." Then there was the coach who was "arrested for assaulting a taxi driver while calling him Bin Laden and other racial slurs."

3. Willingness to dare

So you have the passion and now the knowledge. But neither amounts to much unless you also are willing to dare—to commit, to do the dastardly deed and risk possible criticism or censure.

Yale's sign-pranking of Harvard actually had a historical precedent. Students from the Massachusetts Institute of Technology engineered a similar stunt years before that, passing out cards to the Harvard cheering section at a football game. When the unknowing Harvards flipped over the cards, they spelled out "M-I-T." The "We suck" Yalies gave credit to MIT for inspiring their spoof.

But both Yale and MIT had at least one thing in common: the willingness to stick their necks out. Heckling is like playing the party game "Truth or Dare." It can be embarrassing, awkward, and revealing (not in a good way). It also can be entertaining and full of unexpected pleasures.

But only if you play.

One reassuring aspect of a crowd chant is that you are not alone; you are with your brothers- and sisters-in-arms. Seton Hall's basketball program a few years ago moved its student cheering section at the Prudential Center closer to the visiting team's bench, putting Pirate opponents more directly in the line of fire. Asked if this meant that visiting teams would hear more heckling from Seton Hall students, Associate Athletic Director Jamison Hannigan replied, "Absolutely." He said he encouraged it. "It's a part of gamesmanship."

A university student group, Hall's Hecklers, created a Facebook page to recruit more hecklers and to encourage a sense of community among those who do it. There is a sweet scene in *Ferris Bueller's Day Off* when Ferris (Matthew Broderick) and his buddy Cameron (Alan Ruck) are watching a Chicago Cubs game in the bleachers at Wrigley. Both are high school

Who would have thought that a thing that puts some people off can also bring them together?

students who are cutting class that day and Cameron, finally beginning to perk up after being down in the dumps earlier, starts saying a vintage chant done by all Little Leaguers of a certain time:

"Hey batter batter batter," he says. "Swinggggg batter!"

The object is to get the man at the plate to swing at a bad pitch, but the camera doesn't go to the action on the field. Instead it stays on Cameron and Ferris, who joins his pal in the chant. "Hey batter batter batter. Swinggggg batter!" they say together. Who would have thought that a thing that puts some people off can also bring them together?

4. Tradition

"Hey batter batter . . ." is a golden oldie (or moldy oldie) of baseball heckling—of which there are so many. One is the "He's a bum!" call-and-response chant. Picking out members of the opposing team, the instigator yells, "What's the matter with [name of player]?" The crowd responds, "He's a bum!" Then the instigator yells, "What's the matter with [a second player]?" The crowd says the same: "He's a bum!" And so on down the lineup. As venerable as this chant is, it still gets everyone involved and having fun, including kids.

"At AT&T Park," says one San Francisco Giants fan, "our bullpen warm-up areas are right out on the field. The fans will, in unison, yell 'Whooop' (pitch rising toward the end) whenever the pitcher throws to the warm-up catcher. When the catcher returns it, everyone yells 'Whooo' with the pitch

English soccer chanting and swearing

Those more refined persons who think American sports fans and hecklers swear too much should spend some time in the pubs, community halls, and stadiums frequented by the Premier League fans of Great Britain. English football fans curse quite a bit more than even the most foul-mouthed Americans, and their cursing often finds its way into crowd chants during games. For instance, one English footballer, grabbing the microphone on the stage of a victory celebration for his winning club, said to a crowd of thousands, "What do we think of Tottenham?"

"Sh*t," responded the thousands as one, without prodding.

"And what do we think of sh*t?"

"Tottenham!"

At another match the hometown team was being clobbered 4–0—in soccer terms, that is a humongous wipeout—but the crowd continued to have a jolly good time, singing out to the winning side, "You've only scored 4, you've only scored 4, you must be sh*t, you've only scored 4."

The English appear somewhat more musical than Americans, making up derisive lyrics based on the tunes for "Que Sera, Sera," "The Lion Sleeps Tonight," and other songs. One such singing chant mocked former midfielder Steve Gerrard, who starred for many years at Liverpool but struggled early in his career to bring a Premiere League championship to the city. Sung to the tune of "If you're happy and you know it, clap your hands"—also popular with American sports fans—it has the added bonus of ending with a vulgarity:

• Have you ever seen Gerrard win the league? [clap clap clap]

• Have you ever seen Gerrard win the league? [clap clap clap]

• Have you ever seen Gerrard

• Have you ever seen Gerrard

• Have you ever seen Gerrard

• Have you f**k!

• [Clap clap clap!]

starting high and dropping at the end. You can hear this going on from pretty much any part of the park."

He adds that he is sure that fans in other parks do similar things, and yes they do. That others have done a thing somewhere else doesn't lessen the enjoyment of it. It may even add to it.

Basketball fans chant "Air-ball! Air-ball!" to mock a fellow who misses everything on a shot. "Brick!"—after a free throw attempt clangs the iron—also has been around forever but, if timed right, still entertains. "MVP! MVP!" has become a popular taunt in recent years. Hometown fans chant it when their guy, who did not win the award, is playing against the guy who *did*, such as when league Most Valuable Player Stephen Curry traveled to Houston to play James Harden and the Rockets in the 2015 NBA playoffs. Houston fans thought their guy deserved the prize, not Curry, and mocked the Warriors guard by chanting "MVP" whenever Harden had the ball and did something special.

Basketball fans—fans in all sports, really—will break into spontaneous cheers of "A**hole! A**hole! A**hole!" when a guy wearing the opposing team's jersey walks past them. Polite, no. Kinda funny, yes, as long as you're not that guy.

College basketball crowds like to mix things up—or mix up the guy on the free throw line anyway—by chanting "Block that kick, block that kick" as he's about to shoot. Why do a football chant during a game of hoops? Why not if it makes him miss? One classic crowd heckle is to say "Boink . . . boink . . . pass!" in time as a player dribbles and then passes to a teammate. Michigan State student fans came up with a diabolical way to mess with the opposing team, counting out "6-5-4-3-2-1" as

Blow their minds.

the clock wound down to end a quarter. Trouble was, at least for the visitors, the clock had 12 seconds to go, not 6, and they ended up rushing their shot and missing. Michigan State rebounded the ball and still had time to get down to its basket and score. Another tactic is to start the countdown at a higher number, say, 15 seconds, leading your opponents to think they have plenty of time to shoot. But in reality there are only six seconds left, and the clock runs out while they're still dribbling and they never get a shot up.

Student rooters will receive free college newspapers when they come into the arena so that when the starting lineups for the opposing team are announced, everyone can put the paper in front of their face as if to say, "Who cares? Not us." Then when their team scores a big bucket or goal or wins the game, they rip the papers up and throw the pieces around like confetti.

5. Seizing the opportunity

Tradition matters in heckling. So does recognizing an opportunity and seizing it on the spot. Boxing fans wanted a Floyd Mayweather–Manny Pacquiao title fight and had clamored for one for years. They were the two top fighters in the world at their weight and yet they had never met in the ring. As negotiations to finally hold the match were initiated, Mayweather showed up courtside at the Staples Center in Los Angeles to see the Clippers play. Fans lobbied him directly and loudly with chants of "We want Pacquiao! We want Pacquiao!" Sports fans did indeed get their wish: The two champions eventually fought, with Mayweather winning a deeply disappointing match.

This is not to say that the heckling at Staples goaded Mayweather into agreeing to the fight. Nonetheless, when he ventured outside the bubble world inhabited by elite professional athletes, L.A. fans made sure he knew what they thought. They saw an opportunity and jumped on it.

So it was when Alex Rodriguez, star third baseman for the New York Yankees and a married man, was seen, repeatedly, in different cities around the United States and Canada attending strip clubs with a curvaceous blond stripper who was not his wife. People, including Alex's wife, knew about this because his picture appeared with the stripper online and in the sports pages of tabloid newspapers. To make amends, A-Rod went shopping with his wife at the Ritz Carlton Hotel in Boston and bought her two diamond necklaces worth thousands. This act of marital devotion—also reported in the tabs—occurred the day before he and the Yankees were set to start a three-game series against the Boston Red Sox at Fenway Park.

While all this was playing out, some Red Sox fan or fans got an idea. A wonderful awful idea, as Dr. Seuss might have said. Wonderful to the Red Sox, awful to Rodriguez, for when he showed up for the game hundreds of Fenway fans wore masks over their faces. The masks resembled a certain blond stripper—a cartoon version of her anyhow, with bright yellow hair like Betty in the old Archie comics. A-Rod clearly had a thing for blondes. Witness his earlier affair with Madonna, which also served as fodder for opportunistic hecklers who brought pictures of her to the park and held them up for the Yankee to see when he came to bat. (Another, unrelated tactic of fans whose home team is losing badly and they cannot bear to watch: wearing paper bags over their heads.)

6. A catchy hook

The hook is everything. It is the grabber, what draws people in. It can be verbal or nonverbal yet it is instantly understood. The stripper masks were a kind of hook; people got it, no explanation needed. The whistling that begins the "Potvin sucks" chant—that is another type of hook. The initiator does not yell, "Hey everybody, let's do the 'Potkin sucks' chant." That's too boring. Somebody does the whistles and that is what people listen for and respond to. That's the grabber.

Hooks are catchy; if they weren't, they wouldn't be hooks. "Rock 'n' Roll Part 2" has built-in musical hooks that get people going with the rhythm of the beat, which is essential for effective chanting. The best chants steadily build and build until they're speeding down the track like a diesel locomotive. The chants done by student rooting sections have that sort of industrial-strength intensity, power, and excitement.

Arguably the best student chant, and there are many variations of it, is the "winning team–losing team" chant, performed most famously by Utah State students at Smith Spectrum in Logan. (Search for this chant as well as their "I believe" number on YouTube.) The student leader begins with a simple question, pointing to the scoreboard of a game in progress: "Is that not a scoreboard?" The student section instantly responds, "Yes, that is a scoreboard." The leader next asks, "Is that not a 68?" referring to how many points Utah State has. "Yes, that is a 68," say the students. Then the leader asks how much the other team has. "Is that not a 56?" Again the students answer in the affirmative: "Yes, that is a 56."

The leader then points to Utah State and asks, "Is that not the winning team?" Students: "Yes, that is the winning team."

Now the leader points to the visitors: "Is that not the losing team?" Students: "Yes, that is the losing team." Having done his job, the leader steps aside for the students, who have been pointing to each thing in turn as they have been saying it. Each student in all the student sections across the arena starts jumping up and down in place and pointing first to Utah State, then to the visitors, pointing back and forth again and again as they all chant in unison, "Winning team! Losing team! Winning team! Losing team!" Utah State has one of the best home floor records in NCAA basketball and it is easy to see why.

7. An Us against Them attitude

When you talk about success in major college basketball today, one school always comes to the fore. It also has the loudest, rowdiest, heckling-est student cheering section any-where. Coincidence? Maybe, maybe not. But there can be little dispute that the Cameron Crazies of Duke University are, as writer Al Featherston says, "the standard by which all other college student rooting sections are judged."

Now, this statement will surely irritate many people who dislike the Durham, North Carolina, university and its five-time national championship basketball squad coached by Mike Krzyzewski. The Blue Devils are the New York Yankees or Dallas Cowboys of the schoolboy game; people either love them intensely or hate them intensely, which brings up the seventh and final characteristic of effective group heckling: an attitude of Us against Them. This attitude is hardly exclusive to Duke (or the Yankees or Cowboys); most every sports team, pro or amateur, has it to some degree, as do their fans. The feeling of: We're all in this together, the world doesn't understand us, in fact the world is actively opposing us. But we're all going to stick together and despite the bad luck and injuries and overwhelming odds against us, victory will be ours in the end. And to hell with Them.

This Us against Them attitude crops up all the time with the Cameron Crazies and Duke basketball. "Us" being Duke and "Them" being the anti-Duke contingent, here are some of the incidents that have irritated the hell out of both sides over the years. And just to be contrary, let's begin with Them.

THEM

Tyler Lewis was a short (5-foot-11) guard for North Carolina State whose 83-year-old grandmother had recently died. When he arrived for a game at Cameron Indoor Stadium (Duke's home arena, hence the name the Cameron Crazies), students besieged him with taunts of "Bilbo Baggins," a reference to the character in *The Hobbit* whom the elfish Lewis somewhat resembles, and "Past your bedtime!"—also a jab at his size and his youthful appearance.

So far so good. All's fair in love and heckling. Nothing out of bounds here. But a controversy stirred when it was alleged that a small group of Crazies chanted, "How's your Grandma? How's your Grandma?" at the still-grieving Lewis.

Lewis's teammate at North Carolina State, Richard Howell, said he heard the chant, and he tweeted after the game, "He lost his grandma and y'all chant that? Cowards." Lewis's father said he heard the chant too but that it was only a few students, and that it was only done once.

The accusations caused Duke officials to look into the matter; they interviewed fans and journalists who were there and reviewed the TV tape. They said it was a misunderstanding, or a mishearing to be more accurate. The students were chanting "Past your bedtime," which in the raucous din of the arena some mistakenly heard as "How's your Grandma?"

"What has become clear is that there was no organized chant by the Cameron Crazies referencing Tyler Lewis' grandmother, nor was there any reference to his grandmother's recent passing on the standard cheer sheets that are distributed among the students prior to each game," said a Duke spokesman.

US

While the Crazies may not have "referenced" Lewis's grandmother in their chants, no one disputes that they were all over him for his size or lack thereof. Being short of stature, in basketball terms, is a sure attention-getter at Cameron Indoor Stadium. Whenever Virginia's 5-foot-10 Ricky Stokes shot free throws, the Crazies would yell, "Stand up, Stokes, stand up!" They called tiny Mugsy Bogues of Wake Forest "Webster," a goof on the little boy played by Emmanuel Lewis in the TV show of the same name. And when a diminutive guard for the Australian national team showed up for an exhibition at Cameron, the Crazies greeted him with calls of "Shrimp on the barbie." Now dated but clever back then, this referred to a line by

The Cameron Crazies do indeed produce scouting reports on opposing players.

Paul Hogan of *Crocodile Dundee* fame, who, in TV commercials promoting Australian tourism, invited Americans to visit Down Under, promising that if they did, he'd keep a shrimp on the barbie for them.

US

As for the "standard cheer sheets" alluded to by the Duke investigators in the Tyler Lewis incident, the Cameron Crazies do indeed produce scouting reports on opposing players, although officials may be selling them short, because these sheets are anything but standard. They can be pretty wicked documents, such as the one they did a few years ago about the University of North Carolina, which, along with NC State, is one of Duke's most bitter rivals. "Cheer loudly during time-outs," the instructions, uncovered by ESPN's Darren Rovell, said. "Hex the Carolina huddle if you have to. They shouldn't be able to hear anything in their timeout. Nothing."

Edgier and funnier were the evaluations of individual UNC players. J. P. Tokoto, said the notes, was "known for his ability to dunk the ball really hard once every 17 games, and that's about it." Brice Johnson was "really, really bad at basketball." And Reggie Bullock "prefers his name to be pronounced 'Bull-lock' so obviously disregard this and call him 'Bull-luck' like any normal person would do."

THEM

Such dissing of players is not fair and not necessarily accurate. But it hardly matters because that's not the point. The point is to get under the skin of your opponents. And this cuts both ways, both for and against Duke.

One of Duke's greatest players was Christian Laettner, a brash, superbly talented power forward who excited the Duke haters like no one else before or since. "Laettner, you suck," "Hope you die," and "Hope you go to hell" were only a few of the nasty things he heard in a career highlighted by two NCAA national titles and 13 seasons in the pros. While he was at Duke rumors about his alleged homosexuality—he now has a wife and kids—circulated around campuses and these rumors spurred one rival student section to chant epithets at him such as "Ho-mo-sexual" and "Fag-got, fag-got, fag-got."

"Ninety nine percent of it is fun," Laettner told ESPN when asked if the heckling ever got to him. "But every now and then you get someone who is too rude and crude."

US

Did someone say rude and crude? The Cameron Crazies will take a little of that action. "The refs, they suck, they really really suck," was one of their favorite cheers from years ago. Jay Bilas, a former Duke star who is now a broadcaster, recalls how the Crazies treated referee Dick Paparo. "When Dick Paparo would come in and make a bad call," says Bilas, "they'd chant, 'You suck, Dick! You suck, Dick!'" But then Coach K would get mad at the Crazies and tell them to knock it off, at which point they'd change their chant to "You suck, Richard! You suck, Richard!"

THEM

At a Duke away game, University of Maryland student rooters wore T-shirts that said "F**k you, J. J." and made similar obscene chants to Duke guard J. J. Redick, spinning off on the last syllable of his name.

A few years after that, another Duke guard, Greg Paulus, heard chants of "Teabag Paulus, Teabag Paulus" from the Virginia Tech cheering section, "teabag" being a euphemism for a sexual act. The chants came while Paulus was on the free throw line and they were loud enough to be heard easily on the TV broadcast. "I don't think there's been a Duke guard that hasn't heard what he's hearing," said one of the announcers. "The Bobby Hurleys, the J. J. Redicks—you name it."

US and THEM

One of the most outrageous incidents in Cameron heckling history occurred in 1984 when the Crazies yelled "Rape! Rape!" at the University of Maryland's Herman Veal, who had just been charged with sexually assaulting a coed. They threw hundreds of girls panties at him on the court and one student's sign read, Hey Herman, did you send her flowers?

This brought an instant reaction from Krzyzewski and Duke authorities, who said that the Crazies had overdone it again and that they needed to be better behaved—or else. At the very next game at Cameron, against North Carolina, the Crazies did their best to comply, wearing halos made of clothes hangers and wrapped with aluminum foil. They bore signs that read Welcome, Honored Guests and for the Tar Heel's head coach, A Hearty and Warm Welcome to Dean Smith. Instead of stomping and screaming when a North Carolina player shot a free throw, they held up small, exceedingly polite signs saying Please Miss.

Their good behavior even extended to referee Dick Paparo. "The first time Paparo blew a call," said Al Featherston, "instead of chanting 'Bullsh*t,' the chant was 'We beg to differ.'"

US

Other schools get irritated because many Duke students act as if their education is superior to all and that when it comes to the distribution of IQ in the world, they have a monopoly. One of the signs North Carolina's players saw when they came to Cameron after the Herman Veal game was WELCOME, FELLOW SCHOLARS. If a word on a sign can be said to be dripping with sarcasm, "scholars" was it. Another Duke sign poked at NC State: THEN GOD SAID 'I NEED A PLACE TO TRAIN FARMERS.' SO GOD MADE NC STATE. And: THIS IS OUR HOUSE. GO BACK TO YOUR BARN.

As annoying as this attitude is, the Cameron Crazies produce some seriously comic things. When Florida State's Nigel Dixon, a 7-foot, 350-pound center, came to town they shouted, "Please don't eat me" and tossed a box of Chicken McNuggets onto the court that was attached to a string held by a Duke rooter on the other end. They were hoping Dixon would try to get the McNuggets, at which point they would pull the box away and make him chase it across the court. It didn't work. He wouldn't bite.

Another former big body in college basketball, Shaquille O'Neal, played at Cameron when he was at LSU and he heard chants like "Shaq's got a big ol' butt, oh yeah!' and "Boom shaqalaka, boom shaqalaka," a nice nod to Sly and the Family Stone's epic old-school hit, "I Want to Take You Higher."

North Carolina State forward Lorenzo Charles was accused of stealing from a pizza deliveryman, prompting the Crazies to toss empty pizza boxes onto the court. When two more Wolfpack players got busted for changing the price tags on underwear at a department store, the Crazies lifted a page from

Accused of robbing a pizza guy, Lorenzo Charles was showered with pizza boxes.

their Herman Veal playbook and tossed underpants at them. Then there was center Tom Burleson, who was serenaded to the tune of The Who's "Pinball Wizard" after news broke that he had busted up a pinball machine.

Continuing on with the undergraduate crime report, Notre Dame's Adrian Dantley had an off campus run-in with police that led to his arrest. When he came to the free throw line after being fouled, just before he was about to shoot, the Crazies behind the basket jumped to their feet and shouted, "Freeze! Police!"

US and THEM

The Crazies do not just go after student-athletes; they take on coaches too—and their wives. (At least they used to.) The wife of NC State coach Norm Sloan occasionally sang the national anthem at center court for Wolfpack games in Raleigh. A male Cameron Crazy in drag parodied her by doing the same before a game in Durham, a stunt that so enraged Sloan that he called the Duke student section a bunch of drunken idiots. Next time the Wolfpack came to town, the Crazies sang out rowdy renditions of "100 Bottles of Beer on the Wall" and pretended to drink from oversize plastic beer bottles. Sloan was not a fan.

Nor was Maryland's Lefty Driesell. The Crazies mocked him by coming to games in the same kind of garish sport coats he wore and skullcaps to mimic his bald head. Some of the skullcaps had a gas gauge design on them with the needle pointing to empty, implying that Lefty had less than a full tank when it came to brains. When Driesell broke his ankle and showed up with a cast on his leg, a few of the Crazies wore bad sport coats, skullcaps, *and* fake ankle casts.

Driesell showed good humor, though, playfully standing in front of the student section at Cameron and running a comb over his bald pate. The Crazies loved it. He also led them in games of Simon Says, and after the Herman Veal incident, when asked by a reporter if he had seen the sign about Veal sending the girl flowers, Lefty replied, "No, I can't read. I went to Duke."

US

The greatest Cameron Crazies stunt ever? Well, some say it was the time Steve Hall, a North Carolina guard, came to Duke and sat on the visitors' bench in his street clothes. The reason for this was that less than two weeks earlier, he had been hospitalized with a collapsed lung. Although the condition was not life threatening, he had to stop playing for a while and watch the games from the bench.

The Crazies knew all this, of course, having done their research. Still, they were not going to let up on the Tar Heel player, chanting in slow rhythmic tones, "In-hale, ex-hale, in-hale, ex-hale . . ." It wasn't bitter, it wasn't mean, it was pure jest. Hall, breathing in and out on the bench, allowed himself a smile.

CHAPTER 10

The Green Men, Little SAS, and other costumed characters

Then there was Speedo Guy. Also considered to be one of the most memorable moments in the Cameron Crazies' pantheon, Speedo Guy made his one and only appearance against North Carolina in an ACC conference game at Cameron Indoor Stadium. It was early in the game, and the Crazies were doing their usual wild and crazy thing behind the visitors' basket, standing and yelling, standing and chanting, standing and rattling the rafters with noise.

Then the craziest thing of all occurred. They sat down.

All the Crazies sat down as Jackie Manuel, a Tar Heel swingman, came to the line to shoot two free throws after being fouled. Normally the Crazies do not sit down for any reason but in this case, egged on by Mullet Man (sunglasses, headband, Duke jersey, fake retro mullet) and Viking Guy (in a Norse helmet that would have made Leif Erickson proud), they followed the plan. The plan was for the Crazies to sit down and be quiet the second time a North Carolina player came to the free throw line. That player was Manuel.

As all this was occurring, a Duke undergrad named Patrick King dropped down in his seat and started shedding his pants and shirt. "I wanted it to be something like a blooming flower," said King, describing the impression he wished to make. The last piece of clothing to go was an overcoat, leaving him dressed only in a blue Speedo swimsuit, nothing else.

Per the plan, King's seat was directly in the line of sight of the man at the free throw line, namely Manuel, who did indeed see him rising up from his seat doing his best blooming flower impersonation. "I saw this guy in a Speedo, no shirt, just dancing around," said Manuel, now an assistant coach at UNC Greensboro. "It was kinda hard to focus on my free throws."

Exactly! That was precisely the point and it worked: His first shot clanked off the back rim, and the Speedo Guy and the Crazies exulted in triumph.

Ah, but there was one shot left, the all-important second shot. Manuel had a chance to foil Speedo Guy and redeem himself; all he had to do was make his second free throw because the point of the stunt, after all, was to make him screw up. If he made even one it would mean that a doofus in a swimsuit had wiggled his butt around in the Duke graduate student section, nothing more.

Manuel gathered himself, and as King—now a church pastor—did the equivalent of a pole dance without the pole, up went his shot. This one had better carry than the first but the result was the same. A miss.

The free throw-altering Speedo Guy.

Bedlam ensued. King immediately dropped back down in his seat and threw his clothes on, thus avoiding being kicked out of the arena. The hammer came down after the game from Coach K, who said that although he loved the Crazies and generally supported them, "I don't think you should run around in your underwear." Duke's blooming flower wilted after a single game, never to be seen again.

But Speedo Guy's short, happy life hardly represents the beginning or end of anything in college sports, which remains full of costumed characters. Every Duke home game features shirtless Cameron Crazies with their chests and faces painted blue. Others wear blue man suits, blue wigs, blue towels, blue turbans. Still more wear basketballs on their head, clown suits, Storm Trooper gear. But this is no different than what they do in the Riot Squad (Rutgers), the Zoo (University of Pittsburgh), the Wildside (Northwestern), the Grateful Red (Wisconsin), Cyclone Alley (Iowa State), the Rowdy Reptiles (Florida), the ZonaZoo (Arizona), The Bench (Cal Berkeley), and other student rooting sections. They too paint themselves and dress up in school colors, make noise, and try to get the Jackie Manuels of their world to lose focus. Wild Bill of Utah State has come to games as Peter Pan, the Little Mermaid, and a teacup from *Beauty and the Beast*.

University and arena officials monitor all these student sections for offensive or inappropriate behavior. Also closely watched are the student bands, which can sometimes say or do the wrong thing even when they're not trying to. Look what happened to the Kansas State marching band at a September 2015 football game. Half of the band created a formation on the field that resembled a Jayhawk, the mascot of rival Kansas. Then the other half formed the Starship Enterprise from *Star Trek*—or what it thought was the Starship Enterprise anyhow. To those watching on TV it looked more like a giant penis inserting itself into the mouth of the Jayhawk. Twitter lit up with pictures and comments, and deeply embarrassed K-State bandleaders apologized for their inadvertent mistake.

The instantaneous, overwhelming reaction of social media to faux pas of this or any other kind is partly why universities and athletic conferences crack down on school bands and student rooting sections. "It's hard to do anything," one University of Cincinnati band member complained to NPR during a March Madness game, "because the NCAA staff keeps us from standing up and doing what we normally do." The NCAA put a lid on the Bearcat band's activities during March Madness not because it had done anything wrong but because it *might*. The annual tournament that determines college basketball's best team makes hundreds of millions of dollars every year for the NCAA, its member universities and their athletic departments, the TV networks that broadcast it, and many others. Nobody, least of all basketball fans, wants these games sullied by off-court student hijinks.

Are student rooting sections, then, less rowdy today? Is there less heckling than in the past? Some think so. Others think that some of the chants and comic shtick have been done so much, for so long, they've gotten stale and lost their edge. How many times can you don a Speedo and prance around at a game? Only once at Duke, as it turned out.

The same pressures on colleges are at work in professional sports, inhibiting heckling and rowdy fan behavior. Even so, there is only so much that authorities can do to tamp down on the irrepressible human spirit, especially when it is buoyed by a cocktail or two. At the Olympic Club in San Francisco, Bob Costas was interviewing Webb Simpson live on NBC-TV after Simpson had just won the U.S. Open golf tournament. The two men were standing on a picture-perfect spot on the picture-perfect course when a man in a bird hat stepped in front of

The heckler's best tool

Aclever costume and props are can't miss attention-getters for a heckler. But the best tool in the heckler's toolbox is his or her voice. Here are five tips on how to be sure your voice is always heard.

1. Use what you got. "To sing," wrote Henry Miller, "you must first open your mouth." This is true for heckling as well. You may not be blessed with the pipes of Gilbert Gottfried or Eddie Vedder. No matter. Just open your mouth and let 'er fly.

2. Be there. Speaking up is important, of course—Teller of Penn and Teller would not make a good heckler—but it doesn't matter how loud you are if you do not actually go to the park to see the games. "The more the players see you and hear you," advises Harry the Heckler, a well-known heckler at San Diego Padres games, "the more effect you'll have on them." Harry once saw Barry Bonds of the San Francisco Giants massaging a sore thigh with his hand in the outfield at Petco Park. He shouted, "Barry you're not hurt. You're just using that as an excuse to play with yourself in public."

3. Listen. A key part of making yourself heard in heckling, oddly enough, is being quiet and listening. Another tip from Harry the Heckler: "Wait for the crowd noise and stadium music to die down. Yell very loudly. Keep it clean."

4. Let them hear you . . . a lot. "If you get in the game," one Baltimore heckler told an opposing pitcher warming up in the bullpen, "I want you to think about me. That way we'll clobber your a**. You just keep thinking about me." If you want a player to think about you and keep thinking about you, there is no substitute for persistence—delivering a steady stream of patter, at high volume, over a period of time.

5. Get others to join you. A group of hearty hecklers yelling, "It's all your fault, it's all your fault" to a goalie after he has let in a goal will always carry more impact than one man alone. But enlisting others to join your cause is another way to use your voice—as a leader.

them and started making tropical bird sounds. "Caw-caw-caw-caw," he said. His hat was red, white, and blue and had ruffles on top with a tiny Australian flag logo on it. Perhaps his drink of choice was Foster's; in any case he was having the time of his avian life until a security man in a suit yanked him off camera like the old-time vaudeville bit where the song and dance man gets pulled off stage by his neck with a cane.

Costas and Simpson handled this bit of unscripted silliness with ease. "Always something to spice matters up," Costas said as the man flew off. "Enjoy the jail cell, pal," said Simpson with a laugh.

Want to get attention as a heckler? Wear a bird hat or chicken suit. Another way to get attention is to dress up as Santa Claus and heckle LeBron James. One guy did this at an NBA Christmas Day game, sitting behind the basket and making noise as LeBron shot a pair of free throws. Only he wasn't your cherubic *Miracle on 34th Street* Kris Kringle; he was more like Billy Bob Thornton's Bad Santa. His Santa suit was disheveled and his white hat looked like something a Russian Cossack might wear. His fake beard was pulled down below his chin and he was drinking a beer. The camera fixed on him, and former New York Knicks coach Jeff Gundy, who was broadcasting the game on TV, broke into laughter. "That's a bitter Santa right there. He's not bringing good cheer," he said.

Santa is a Christmastime staple for sports arena costume-wearers, including Canada's Green Men, two of the funniest and best hecklers in the business today. The Green Men wear green spandex bodysuits somewhat similar to the Blue Man Group of performance theater fame. The Green Men are a performance group too, only their routines involve heckling ice hockey players who land in the opposing team's penalty box at Rogers Arena in Vancouver, the home ice of the NHL Vancouver Canucks. The Green Men have become so popular that the Canucks use them to attract fans to come to games. "See the Green Men Live," says a Canucks online advertisement for an upcoming game. As of late 2015 the Green Men had more than 50,000 Twitter followers and nearly 200,000 Facebook likes. Subway and Pepsi hire them to promote their products. They make personal appearances at hockey arenas in Canada and the United States. Before matches in Vancouver they pose for pictures with fans, particularly young children who dress up in Green Men costumes for Halloween. The Green Men have done what would have been unthinkable in an earlier day: They have made a business out of heckling and are turning a profit from it.

The Green Men try to keep their identities secret, which they are able to do to some degree because their suits cover their face and entire body. They are a duo and go by the name of Force (he's the taller one, in the light green suit) and Sully (shorter, in darker green). Besides their physical comedy they have a lively wit that showed itself in their Santa Claus routine in a December game against the visiting Toronto Maple Leafs.

"Green Men" Force and Sully, hockey's unique penalty-box hecklers.

Force had on a Santa hat and white beard and Sully was in a red Santa jacket, and they brought along a large sign with the names of all the Leaf players on it. Next to each name was a blank box, and the two green Santas were checking the boxes to see who had been naughty or nice.

The referees whistled Leafs defenseman Mike Komisarek for interference, and he took his seat in the visitors' penalty box to serve his three minutes of penalty time. This was when Sully and Force—sitting right next to the penalty box in Row 1, C13 and Row 2, C13, one seat directly behind the other—went to work, pulling out Santa's list and pressing it against the glass next to Komisarek's face to get him to look at it. Force found the player's name on the sign and yes, he'd been naughty, so he checked the box with a black marking pen.

While doing this little bit the Green Men kept moving. They are never stationary. "Stationary" is a word that should never be used in connection with them. They climb up and down and alongside the sin box's glass wall "like monkeys in trees," as *Pardon the Interruption*'s Tony Kornheiser says. They twitch and gyrate their pelvises with Elvis-like abandon. They dance and shake their booties. They press their spandex-covered faces against the glass. They hold up cardboard standees of hockey fan/movie star Vince Vaughn. They do boo-hoo crybaby routines to make the opposing player feel bad that he's been temporarily thrown off the ice and has hurt his team. They stand on their heads and shake their crotches in front of his face at just about eye level (glass wall separating them, of course). They do reverse handstands and press their butts against the glass. They produce a big box of Eggo waffles and start tossing the waffles helter-skelter in the air after pretending to bite into them.

Meanwhile the long-suffering Canuck fans—their team has never won a Stanley Cup and is a perennial also-ran—go nuts. They relish the screwball spectacle of it all, cheering the greenies on to greater and greater heights of ludicrousness. As for the player in the box, he mostly tries to ignore the Green Men, although this is an impossibility because of the Rogers Arena fans who are standing and cheering and Eggo-ing their costumed heroes on. Sometimes a player grudgingly acknowledges what is going on and may even laugh. Others angrily stick a glove over the penalty box camera to prevent their faces and their reactions from being shown on TV and in the arena.

"We try to get into the players' heads, and if you can get into the players' heads and just screw with them a little bit," Force told an interviewer, "you can knock 'em out of the zone. It's hard to get back in there." That's the goal of every heckler—to knock an opposing player out of the zone—and the Green Men do that as well as entertain the fans, same as the Phillie Phanatic and other costumed mascots in major league baseball.

The Phanatic has long been a mainstay of Philadelphia baseball and is the official mascot of the Phillies. A sort of fatter and greener version of Big Bird with a strange, tube-like nose and clown shoes, he wears a white Phillies home jersey over his neon green fur. His job includes heckling visiting players and managers. One of the most infamous examples of this was when he got into a serious tussle with Tommy Lasorda, who was then managing the Los Angeles Dodgers. The Hall of Fame manager, who famously bled Dodger blue, did not appreciate the fact that between innings the Phanatic was slapping and making fun of a dummy wearing a Dodgers cap and uniform.

This was in Veterans Stadium, the old home of the Phillies, and Lasorda marched out of the dugout with one purpose in mind: to stop the Phanatic and get that dummy away from him. The Phanatic, who may have thought Lasorda was only fooling around, comically backpedaled away from him. But Lasorda was not fooling around. He grabbed an ATV that the Phanatic had been riding on and started to push it away. The Phanatic

The Phillie Phanatic took a beanball from the Dodgers dugout.

took a few steps closer to Lasorda and stuck out his belly in a pantomime of the portly manager. This ticked off Lasorda even more; he ran after the mascot and finally caught him at third base, knocking him down and grabbing the dummy and socking him with it.

His mission complete, Lasorda returned to the dugout with the dummy in hand. No more was that thing going to be part of this game. Still, not willing to abandon his shtick just yet, the Phanatic hopped back on the ATV and rode it tauntingly in front of the visitors' dugout, at which point a baseball—thrown hard—came firing out of the dugout and hit him in his side. Finally realizing this was no joke to the Dodgers, he rapidly drove away.

Another celebrated encounter between a costumed team mascot and a player or manager occurred when Charles Barkley pretend-punched "Super Mascot" Rocky of the Denver Nuggets and pretend-kicked him on the floor. The two had several such run-ins over the years, all done in the spirit of laughs, unlike the Lasorda incident. Another time Rocky, borrowing a gag from the old-time heckler playbook, sat on the court in a folding chair, reading a newspaper as the visiting Los Angeles Lakers were introduced before a game in Denver. Rocky could not be bothered to look up as Kobe Bryant and the other starters jogged onto the court. The Lakers played along, surrounding Rocky in their team huddle and bouncing around him while he still sat in his chair.

Super Mascot Rocky, the Phillie Phanatic, and the Green Men all point to an inconvenient truth about heckling: The teams and leagues don't mind hecklers as long as they can control them and they contribute to the product they are

The unhappy heckler

Rob Szasz is a case study in how fortunes can change for hecklers. Known as the Happy Heckler—he even wrote a self-published memoir with this title—he became a popular fixture at Tropicana Field, rooting for his beloved Tampa Bay Rays and rooting against whomever they were playing. He insulted the opposition without attacking them personally or resorting to profanity.

Once, when Toronto's John McDonald came up to bat, in a clever play on his last name Szasz sang out, "E-I-E-I-O!" Another time, with Michael Saunders at the plate, he did a similar riff based on the player's last name: "What's it gonna be, Colonel Sanders? Extra crispy or original? Where's the little red and white bucket, baby? Leave it back in the dugout? Let's see you swing that drumstick, Colonel."

There was no mistaking Szasz's croaking frog of a voice in mostly deserted Tropicana Field. These were the years when the Rays lost far more than they won, and the club relished having a happy heckler in its midst. His car license plates read "HCKLR" and he did promotions and ads for the Rays to get people to join him at the park.

When at last Tampa Bay became a winning team, more fans started coming out to Tropicana. Some of them, however, did not like this man in the black wig and fake beard—yes, he occasionally wore costumes too—sitting around home plate, insulting players with that irritating voice of his. They complained. They thought it was rude. Some people watching at home on TV—there were more of those too, with the Rays' success—also heard him during the broadcasts shouting from his seat. They did not like it either.

Interviewed by the *Wall Street Journal* about the complaints and how his standing at Tropicana had changed over the years, Szasz said he was a team guy and that he'd do whatever the Rays wanted. "Everything I do I basically do for the team," he said. "And like I say, if they said stop it, it'd be over in a second." He eventually retired.

selling, ideally helping the teams move tickets. Bruce Reznick is, as he proclaims himself, "the No. 1 Brooklyn Nets fan in the world." He sits behind a basket at the Barclays Center in Brooklyn suited up in a white Nets jersey with the numeral 1 and his nickname, "Mr. Whammy," stitched onto the back. The silver-haired, bespectacled Reznick was born and raised in Brooklyn and is old enough to have seen the Brooklyn Dodgers play at Ebbets Field back when the young Tommy Lasorda pitched for the team. Once an enthusiastic Dodgers fan, he has since switched his allegiance—and ageless enthusiasm—to the Nets. But he does not just sit and watch their games; he takes an active part in helping them win, or so he sincerely believes.

"I love my Nets through thick and thin," he told Grantland. "I cheer for them and I make points for them. You think I'm nuts. Everybody thinks I'm nuts. But I truly believe I have that power. And the whammy is the power."

As soon as an opposing player goes to the free throw line, Mr. Whammy bounds from his seat and runs to a spot next to the basketball stanchion. "You gotta miss, you gotta miss," he repeats again and again as the player bounces the ball and readies his shot. Then as the shot goes off Mr. Whammy jumps in the air, shouts "Miss!" and throws a whammy on him, which consists of both his arms raised high, with the pinky finger and index finger of both hands stretched out, and the middle fingers held down by the thumb, his arms and hands and fingers all waving wildly at the end in order to distract the shooter. Mr. Whammy truly believes that his hexes cost whoever the Nets are playing five to eight points per game, and who's to say not? Certainly not the Nets. The last thing they're going to do is crack down on a warm and lovable eccentric who is just having fun. The media does features on him. He's a character. Fans love him.

But when people—and teams and leagues and TV networks—are not quite sure what to make of the heckler, the reaction is considerably different, like when the late Andy Kaufman did his stand-up routine. Was Kaufman actually doing an act, a comic bit, or was he serious? Was he trying to make us laugh, or was he making fun of us? Or both? Audiences couldn't always tell. The same was true for another brilliant, improvisational heckler, or group of them, known as the Stephen A. Smith Heckling Society of Gentlemen. Their target was the broadcaster Stephen A. Smith, whom they mocked outrageously with a hand puppet called "Little SAS," the acronym being formed from the initials of Smith's name.

Smith, known by many simply as Stephen A., is a sports personality and NBA analyst with real journalistic chops, having written for the *Philadelphia Inquirer* before moving into radio and television. He is smart, funny, opinionated, cocky, and self-important (a trait not unknown in broadcasting), and he loves to hear the sound of his own voice (ditto). This made him a target-rich environment for Little SAS, a sock puppet who was voiced and manipulated by an unidentified member of the Society. Others in the group filmed him and acted as protection.

Little SAS made his most prominent appearance during the first round of the 2007 NBA Draft at a room in Madison Square Garden in New York. ESPN was broadcasting the draft live, and Smith and others were commenting on it. They sat on a podium discussing each team's picks as people watched from the audience. One of the audience members was Little SAS, who called out from the back of the room during a commercial break, "Stephen A. Smith, you got your cheese doodles?"

Smith looked up from what he was doing to see where the voice was coming from. It was coming from a man wielding a sock puppet who was doing a very good, one might even say uncanny, impersonation of Smith's voice. He decided to play along. "No," he answered.

"Quite frankly," answered the sock puppet, "you need some cheese doodles."

Cheese doodles was a recurring theme of Little SAS, apparently referring to some comment Smith had made about how he liked them. Though it drew some laughs, this line of questioning did not lead anywhere, and so Little SAS took his act into a hallway in the Garden where NBA draftees passed after learning that a team had selected them.

The first player to appear was University of Florida center Al Horford, who was selected as the third pick overall by the Atlanta Hawks. The hall was mobbed with onlookers and reporters eager to talk to the soon-to-be-wealthy draftees. One of the most eager was Little SAS. "Some people say you're the best forward since Slobber [actually Slava] Medvedenko," he said. "What do you have to say about that? I'm Stephen A. Smith. Everything I say is important."

Horford did not think so, however, and blew right past him. The puppet went on, "Come on, say something to Stephen A. Smith. Quite frankly, this is the biggest outrage I've ever seen. Al Horford, come back here." Still Horford did not stop and Little SAS chased him down the hall. "What are you doing, Al Horford? Billy Donovan would be ashamed of you right now. Quite frankly, this is a disgrace."

Next came Mike Conley Jr., selected fourth overall by the Memphis Grizzlies, who grinned widely but who also did not stop for Little SAS, causing a mini-fit. "I'm Stephen A. Smith. Everything I say is important. Why aren't you talking to me?" When someone asked him what show he was on, he croaked, "I'm from *Quite Frankly*. Haven't you seen the show?"

"Quite frankly" was a pet phrase of Smith's. No such show existed but that did not bother Little SAS, who still could not get any of the players—all swarming with security and hangers-on—to stop. Finally Joakim Noah, the first-round pick of the Chicago Bulls, appeared in the hallway and Little SAS went after him. "Because he has been such a man of the people, and because his hair is so long, I dub thee Joakim Noah, the people's princess." As Noah brushed past him Little SAS came closer to the 6-foot-11, 230-pounder's face. "I'm Stephen A. Smith. You want to talk to me? Can you sign me?"

Noah shoved the puppet out of his way and Little SAS reacted in mock outrage. "Oh oh, don't do that to Stephen A. Joakim Noah has just slapped Stephen A. Smith." Like an actor in the midst of a performance, which he was, Little SAS stayed

Little SAS, the sock puppet who heckled ESPN's Stephen A. Smith.

in character despite being pushed by a very large man in a small space packed with people. But this may have rattled him because he soon went back to the room where Stephen A.—the real Stephen A.—was doing the TV show. If Smith thought he had gotten rid of the annoying little nuisance, he learned otherwise when he stood up during a break to leave the room.

"I think you know what time it is," said Little SAS. "I think it's time for Stephen A. to visit the can." After Smith had returned to the room and sat back down, Little SAS, as always speaking in Smith's voice, pretended to share his thoughts with the commentator next to him. "I can't tell you what I dropped in there but it's bigger than Slobber Medvedenko."

Little SAS made another appearance at the Garden for the 2009 NBA Draft, but in the interim something had clearly changed. Still doing his best Stephen A. improv act, the sock puppet heckler managed to briefly gain access to the hallway where the draftees passed, trying—and failing, of course—to interview No. 1 overall pick Blake Griffin and others. Whether by design or happenstance, he was largely shut out of the action, being forced at one point to interview another costumed character—a buxom, scantily clad woman in Yankee Doodle stars and stripes. "I like Stephen A. Smith of ESPN," she said. "Extra Special People's Network."

This represented the end of Little SAS and the Stephen A. Smith Heckling Society of Gentlemen. The group produced a farewell video in which they said good-bye to the broadcaster and thanked him for putting up with them. "Best of luck to ya, Stephen A.," they said. "God bless." Despite the nice sentiments Stephen A. Smith never commented publicly on the hecklers, and it is a safe bet he was happy to see them go.

CHAPTER 11

"You cannot be serious:" A plan to save tennis

E ven if they regarded them as unfunny and impolite, most Americans, including Stephen A. Smith, would say that the men behind Little SAS have the right to free speech under the Constitution. But do they have the right to heckle? This may be more of an open question than one might think.

"Is a heckler protected by the First Amendment?" asked reporter Linton Weeks in an analysis for NPR. "This is up for debate." One thing also agreed upon by most, including First Amendment advocates, is that Little SAS did not have what is known as "the heckler's veto." This is a legal term that describes a person who disrupts a speaker at an event and tries to stop him from speaking, thereby denying the speaker's free speech rights as well as the rights of those who were assembled to hear him. Little SAS did nothing like this, of course, and never interfered with anyone's rights, although he did irritate plenty of people.

The legality of heckling, according to Weeks, depends "on where and how and why the heckling occurs." He adds, "Heckling at a hockey game is not considered the same as heckling at a campus lecture." (Unfortunately at some colleges today and in politics, the heckler's veto is sometimes tolerated by authorities who allow individuals and small groups to shout down speakers with whom they disagree.) But in sports, hecklers do not have veto power; they cannot legally disrupt a game, and they will not be permitted to do so. The National Lawyers Guild writes, "Although the law is not settled, heckling should be protected unless hecklers are attempting to physically disrupt an event or unless they are drowning out other speakers."

Heckling is part of the tradition of many sports, and fans enjoy it and accept it. But what about a sport that bans it outright? Or if it does not ban it outright, it is viewed with distaste and disapproval. We are referring to tennis, where fans are expected not to make a sound when a player is serving and cheer only after a point is over, or during rallies. When the umpire tells them to shush, they must fall silent or the match may not proceed.

In a serious break with tradition, the Big 12 athletic conference attracted national attention in spring 2015 when it announced that its tennis teams were going to not only permit heckling, but encourage it. "In the Big 12 conference this college tennis season," writes Tom Perrotta in the *Wall Street Journal*, "schools are saying pish-posh to polite crowds and umpires who announce 'Quiet, please!' at the slightest provocation." Student fans at the tennis matches can act like they do in other sports and yell, scream, shout, chant, and say annoying things to the opposing players.

Perrotta reports that one Baylor student screamed, "He's got the yips! He's got the yips!" after a University of Oklahoma player faulted his serve during a match between the two schools. Another fan grunted audibly when a female OU player tried to serve. Another Baylor fan took a more literate approach, reading aloud from an ancient tennis instructional manual to distract the players on the court. Students yelled when a player tossed the ball in the air to serve—a no-no in conventional tennis—and one of the yellers said he had never had so much fun at a tennis match. Heckling in tennis, he said, is "better than football because they can actually hear me when I talk to them."

The Big 12 is a major power Division 1 conference based in the Southwest that includes Baylor and Oklahoma, which have two of the strongest college tennis programs in the

Big 12 fans behaving "under the same principles/guidelines of other sports."

nation. Texas Christian University is another Big 12 school, and it was the Horned Frogs' tennis coach, David Roditi, who lobbied for the rule change to permit heckling. The "Roditi Rule" simply permits tennis fans "to behave under the same principles/guidelines of other sports (no profanity, vulgarity, abusive comments, etc.)." As long as they stay away from YSA and similar abuses, they can act like they do when OU takes on Baylor in a Saturday afternoon football game in Norman. TCU's tennis program now has a student rooting section, Purple Rain, and like student rooting sections everywhere, they occasionally go over the line, such as when an overzealous fan yells "Out!" when a ball hits close to the line but is still in play, unfairly throwing a player off and disrupting the point.

The Big 12 adopted this new heckle-friendly approach to bolster its tennis programs and increase interest in tennis among students. The problem was that undergrads had to act like they were at study hall or in the library when they came to matches. Keep a lid on it, no raising your voice at the wrong times. And if you did speak out of turn, you would be slapped with a warning and your team penalized. The kids are all right. Why not shake things up and let them have some fun? Maybe they'd get a kick out of it and come back and bring their friends with them. This was the thinking behind the change.

Again, as the evidence repeatedly shows, hecklers do not drive fans away; they help bring them in. It's like when you go to a restaurant and there are no other diners there; perhaps it's early in the day or business is slow. What the host or hostess often does is seat you at a table close to the window so that passersby on the street can see people inside enjoying themselves. This encourages them to stop in and eat there too. It is the same with hecklers. They are bodies in the seats. They are loyal. They bring passion and excitement and they care. And they're having a good time! Come on in and join 'em. Won't hurt a bit.

Tennis tradition says that you handle hecklers the way Novak Djokovic did at a Rogers Cup match in Toronto. A heckler sat behind the great Serbian pro, one of the world's best, muttering things to him after every point. It bothered Djokovic but he said nothing until the fan spoke up as Djokovic was serving and he hit the ball out. No longer stoically accepting his fate, he walked over to the heckler and confronted him. "What's your problem?" he said. "You came here to provoke? Is that what you came for?"

Djokovic: You came here to provoke?
Heckler [squeaky voice]: No.

The seething 6-foot-2 champion looked immense on the court and the heckler seemed tiny, even though the heckler was sitting above him in a slightly elevated row of seats. "No," he squeaked.

"So what's your problem? So why are you saying things after every point?"

The heckler kept shrinking like Alice after she ate the pill, saying "Sorry, sorry, sorry." The giant Djokovic walked back

Jimmy Connors: Portrait of an on-the-court heckler

Jimmy Connors and John McEnroe had many things in common. Both were extraordinary tennis champions, winners of Wimbledon and other Grand Slam tourneys, and along with Björn Borg, the best players of their era.

Both were hecklers at heart too, their behavior routinely and deliberately stepping over that imaginary but real entity known as "the line." Said Connors: "Of course I went over the line, no doubt. But that's what it was there for. The line was there to sometimes be crossed."

Cross it he did, slagging officials for their calls—"You are an abortion, you are an abortion," he screamed to them—flipping people off, swearing, screaming, stomping around, pointing his finger, throwing his racquet, pretending to kick an umpire in the butt when the umpire stooped down to pick up a ball. Connors intimidated and scapegoated officials, turning crowds against them and for him, and he fed off this energy to help him beat hard opponents. The most famous instance of this came in the second set of the 1991 U.S. Open when, on the verge of losing to the young Aaron Krickstein, the 39-year-old turned things in his favor by peeling the skin off the chair judge after he overturned a line call. "You can't see a ball right in front of you, let alone over there," he screamed at him, pointing and shouting, "Get out! Get out!" With the fired-up crowd now acting, in sports radio announcer Scott Ferrall's words, "like baboons," Connors came back to win the set and the match.

Perhaps because they were so similar in so many ways, each threatening the other's dominance on the court, Connors and McEnroe hated each other in those days and still aren't exactly chummy. In his first appearance at Wimbledon, the young and chippy McEnroe played Connors in the semifinals, grousing perpetually at the calls he didn't like. During a changeover Connors, seven years older and then the more established star, wagged his finger at Mac and told him, "Keep your mouth shut." As McEnroe grew in stature and became a star, the rivalry grew pricklier still. Whenever the two men played "we trash-talked each other," recalled McEnroe. "Jimmy called me a baby, and I told him what he could kiss."

over to resume the match as the two TV announcers expressed their approval over how the heckler had just been served. "I like how he just came right up, got right in his grill," said one.

"I bet that shut him up a bit too," said the other. "Usually when you confront a guy like that, they back right down. Is that your experience?"

"Yeah," answered the first announcer. "That's the best way. He didn't scream at him or anything. Kept it civil."

Jimmy Connors had tennis fans acting "like baboons."

In ESPN's superb *30 for 30* documentary on Connors, he explained his philosophy of tennis and how he sought to gain an edge on an opponent. "It's amazing," he said. "It takes one shot, one noise, one click, one clap, one boo, one whatever to come in a match and change everything around." No finer expression of the heckler's credo has ever been said.

Tennis fans are not nearly as civil as the sport's genteel reputation and country club traditions might suggest. Big matches in the Davis Cup, an annual international tournament in which players represent their countries and compete as a team, are as rowdy and noisy as Patriots-Jets games. Three of the four stops in tennis's Grand Slam—Roland-Garros for the French Open, Melbourne Park for the Australian Open, and especially Flushing Meadows for the U.S. Open—can be unruly places to play as well. Serena Williams found that out one year at the French when the fans turned on her and she lost an early-round match. "It's hard to get the rhythm," she said. "It's hard to make them stop."

The heckling can come from unexpected quarters too. Mirka Federer, Roger Federer's wife and a former Swiss tennis pro, caused a spat when she heckled her husband's opponent, Stan Wawrinka, during an ATP Tour final in London. After yelling out support for her husband between his first and second serves, another no-no, she made things worse by calling Wawrinka a *pleure bebe*—"crybaby" in French. Wawrinka, a fellow Swede who plays alongside Federer on the country's Davis Cup team, complained to the chair umpire and to Mirka's husband across the net. The two men exchanged heated words after the match but patched things up later.

Mirka Federer's breach of etiquette hardly compares though to the many, many examples of bad behavior over the years by tennis pros, the most notorious of all being John McEnroe, a former No. 1 in the world who was in his time what Djokovic and Federer are in theirs: the best player in the game, or close to it. Now decades past retirement, his thinning gray hair presenting a far different look than when he was young and his thick, curly mop poked above a headband and on both sides below it, he has become a personable and popular TV broadcaster and a major voice on behalf of tennis itself—a game he frequently ridiculed, outraged, and offended in his mop-haired days.

"There was a time—I'll admit it—when my head was so big it barely fit through the door," said McEnroe in his autobiography, and no one who saw him throw tantrums and abuse umpires and linesmen would ever disagree.

His most noxious example of stinky behavior—and there are countless from which to choose—came in 1981 on the hallowed grounds of Wimbledon, tennis's most prestigious, traditional, and well-mannered Grand Slam tournament. But the young McEnroe thought little of tradition or manners, and he put on a show unlike anyone had seen there before, tossing his racquet in the air in disgust and smashing it on the ground and screaming repeatedly at the umpire for what he perceived to be bad calls. During one of these tantrums he delivered a line that has since become his trademark: "Man, you cannot be serious!"

McEnroe hurled a bunch of other insults at the umpire— "You are the absolute pits!" "You are the pits of the world!" "This guy is an incompetent fool!"—all of which shocked the Centre Court audience and delighted young people around the world who identified with his antiestablishment impertinence. The cocky, contemptuous American was tossing a stink bomb into England's national garden party and they loved it. Tennis traditionalists and the London tabloids were less enamored; they ripped "Super Brat" repeatedly and defended the shell-shocked umpire who had penalized him for breaking

Wimbledon's rules by uttering a profanity. Super Brat claimed he did not swear, that this was a misunderstanding—that the umpire thought he had called him "the absolute piss" of the world but what he had said was "pits."

Chrissie Hynde of the Pretenders got it right; she put the phrase "You are the pits of the world" into a song of hers, "Pack it Up," and this line became another McEnroe trademark, along with one he often shouted at tennis officials who had blown a call (in his view): "You're a disgrace to mankind!"

"You're a disgrace to mankind!"

Despite this contretemps McEnroe went on to win Wimbledon that year and two more times after that, a clutch of U.S. Opens—played in his home state of New York—and a slew of other titles. His 1980 men's final at Wimbledon against Björn Borg is regarded as one of the best matches in the long history of the game. For all his accomplishments McEnroe will always be remembered for how frequently his behavior "crossed the line," at Wimbledon and everywhere else. McEnroe himself admitted it, saying, "I went over the line."

Be forewarned, hecklers. Things that professional athletes say and do during games and matches—swearing, name-calling, trash-talking, confronting and abusing officials, giving them the finger, acting ridiculous, being a hothead, throwing things, disrupting play—is off-limits for you. If you "cross the line"—a line that frequently shifts, depending on who is drawing it and who is supposed to abide by it—you will be gone (and rightly so, in many cases). But if you cross the line repeatedly and you are a star, you may become rich.

McEnroe has made millions of dollars making TV commercials and other advertisements that poke fun at his bad boy behavior and all the rotten things he said in the past. "Unbelievable! Toenail fungus? Seriously!" says the one-time hero of rebellious youth in mock anger while promoting a medical remedy for toenail fungus. In another TV spot, this one about banking, he is playing a match against Andy Roddick and smashes a serve that lands near the line. When the umpire calls it out McEnroe explodes in pretend rage: "Wait a minute! You gotta be kidding! The ball was out. Get your eyes checked. Help me out here!" The English apparently have forgiven him for his Wimbledon excesses, because he reprises his "You cannot be serious!" line in an ad for an English firm that insures mobile phones.

In a commercial for a Spanish car company, he gets into a heated dispute with a policeman who is writing him a ticket for parking on the wrong side of a traffic line. McEnroe has just returned from playing tennis, and he says his car is inside the line. "How can you possibly call that? It's clearly in. It's in!" But the officer won't budge and McEnroe delivers more theatrical rage—"You cannot be serious! This is some bullsh*t!"—before breaking his racquet. A spot for Mars candy bars is unique in that it shows actual footage of him playing as a young man, in the heat of a big match, when McEnroe really meant what he was saying and it was not a joke. "You cannot be serious, man," he screams at the ump. "You cannot be serious!"

In yet another commercial, this to encourage the spaying and neutering of pets, McEnroe is talking to a man who refuses to neuter his dog. Later this is revealed to be a misunderstanding, but McEnroe gets upset at the man and trots out, one more time, the hardest-working line in the advertising business. "You cannot be serious!" he says to him. "Neutering is good for his temper."

No doubt many in tennis would scoff at the notion that more heckling is good for the game and might broaden its fan appeal. Bad behavior by fans or players should not be encouraged, they say. Nonetheless, if those enthusiastic student rooters in the Big 12 ever need help with their heckling, we know a good person for them to call. He has lots of terrific insult lines that they can use and maybe even some new ones nobody has heard before. Seriously!

CHAPTER 12

World heckling capital

What makes McEnroe act the way he does, at least when he was a brash young tennis star? If you ask him, it is where he comes from.

"That's the question interviewers always work around to asking me," he wrote in *You Cannot Be Serious.* "How did you get that way? And the first thing I tell them is, I'm a New Yorker. New Yorkers don't hold anything back. We lay it on the line, and we don't whisper when we do it."

All this is true, certainly, but the geographical terrain of hecklers extends far beyond the borders of the Empire State. Jimmy Connors was born and raised in East St. Louis, Missouri. The original Nasty Boy, the man who schooled both Connors and McEnroe on how to antagonize and offend, was Ilie Nastase, a Romanian. Mirka Federer, who stood by her man at that match in London, is Swiss and did her heckling in French.

Of course, under the conventional definition, what McEnroe, Connors, and Nastase did was not heckling—instead they were "talking smack" the way pros do when they go *mano a mano* in an athletic contest. Call it whatever you like, it is still heckling. They grab the heckle tool and scrape, rip, pull apart, and shred their opponents with it. What was Reggie Miller doing to Spike Lee in their famous spat if not heckling him? (Reggie, by the way, is from Los Angeles and Spike is as Brooklyn as they come.) That's different, one might argue, because Reggie was only striking back at Spike, who was trying to mess up his mojo and help the Knicks win. Exactly. That's what hecklers do. Players do the same.

Some of the biggest names in the history of basketball—including Michael Jordan (he grew up in North Carolina) and Larry Bird (the pride of French Lick, Indiana)—were heavy-duty hecklers and trash-talkers. It became as true with the next generation, including Kevin Garnett (South Carolina born), Kobe Bryant (Philadelphia), and others. They beat up on their opponents not only physically but mentally too. Coaches do it as well. All game long they whine and whine to the referees with the aim of getting the calls to go their way, especially at crunch time. Owners get in on the act too.

Dallas Mavericks owner Mark Cuban (Pittsburgh native) sits near the home team's bench when they play in Dallas and often goes on the road with them for playoff games, heckling referees, players, and coaches. This has earned him his share of enmity from opposing fans. "No one takes more abuse and gets more threats on the road than I do," Cuban wrote on his blog. "I've also had my family and friends spit on." His worst moment as a fan and heckler came at home after the Mavs lost a hard-fought playoff game to the Denver Nuggets some years ago. Cuban took the loss as hard as his players, and after the game, in the hallway leading to the locker room, he saw the mother of Kenyon Martin, Denver's rugged power forward. He called the Nuggets "thugs" to her face and said, "That includes your son. Your son is a punk." Cuban later apologized.

Former Los Angeles Clippers owner Donald Sterling went so far as to heckle his own players, sitting courtside and picking on guard Baron Davis in particular. "Why are you in the game?" he would shout at him. "Why did you take that shot? You're out of shape!" Sterling, who has since unwillingly sold the team, lives in Beverly Hills.

From Beverly Hills to Brooklyn, from French Lick to Switzerland, hecklers come in all shapes and sizes, from all walks of life, are male and female, are all colors and ethnicities, and can be found all around the map. Harry the Heckler is San Diego. The Green Men are Vancouver. Dr. Heckle is Salt Lake. Random Jerry is Detroit. The Happy Heckler was Tampa Bay. The Cameron Crazies are Durham. Robin Ficker lives in Maryland. Mr. Whammy is bred-in-the-bone Brooklyn. And those two teenagers who started the Hunter Pence sign craze? New York (or Long Island or New Jersey) all the way, same as the Stephen A. Smith Heckling Society of Gentlemen.

Still, if you took a survey of all the hecklers and trash-talking athletes mentioned in this book—hell, let's go beyond that: Let's expand the survey to every professional athlete, coach, and front office executive in all of professional sports— and asked them, "What is the worst city for heckling?" there is no question that a large majority of them would say one city, and one city above all:

The Iron Lung and other old-time hecklers

Given its reputation, it comes as no surprise that Philadelphia boasts one of the all-time great old-time hecklers, a man by the name of Pete Adelis, known as "the Iron Lung of Shibe Park," which was where the Phillies and the Philadelphia Athletics played back in the old, old days.

Adelis, according to Bruce Nash and Allan Zullo of the *Baseball Hall of Shame* series, "stood six feet tall, weighed 260 pounds, wore a size-52 coat—and owned a booming voice to match." He used that booming voice to such effect that the Yankees occasionally brought him to New York to heckle teams they were playing, similar to how Charles Barkley hired Robin Ficker to clown on Michael Jordan and the Chicago Bulls against Barkley's Phoenix Suns.

Adelis, whose heyday was in the 1940s and '50s, believed, like Ficker, that research was key to effective heckling. His "rules of scientific heckling," first published in 1948 by *The Sporting News* (and posted online by the Baseball Almanac), are as instructive to-day as they were back then: "1. No profanity. 2. Nothing purely personal. 3. Keep pouring it on. 4. Know your players. 5. Don't be shouted down. 6. Take it as well as give it. 7. Give the old-timer a chance—he was a rookie once."

A few other old-time (non-Philly) hecklers:

Hilda Chester. An Ebbets Field mainstay in the days of the 1930s Brooklyn Dodgers, she was, wrote Peter Golenbock, "a plump, pink-faced woman with a mop of stringy gray hair" and a "fish peddler voice." She banged a frying pan with an iron ladle and rang a cowbell. When things got too quiet at Ebbets, the call went out to Hilda for more cowbell.

Leon "The Barber" Bradley. The Barber was also a Detroit heckler, although his beat was basketball. He worked the Cobo Arena and the Palace at Auburn Hills in the Bad Boys era of the Detroit Pistons, sitting behind the visitors' bench and issuing a profanity-laden stream of insults at any team that would dare challenge Isaiah Thomas and Co. One pundit described him as "the uncensored Robin Ficker." Bill Walton, on the sharp edge of the Barber's sarcasm as a center for the Portland Trailblazers and Boston Celtics, called him "the most venomous tongue in NBA history." It is certain that the Barber's foul-mouthed style would not play well in today's somewhat more antiseptic NBA. Away from the arena, he worked with underprivileged young people and had a park named after him.

Philadelphia.

It is the world heckling capital. The city of brotherly love and the Liberty Bell. The home of Ben Franklin, Rocky Balboa, and the Phillie Phanatic. Where they signed the Declaration of Independence and where Hall & Oates inked their first record

Joe "The Brow" Diroff. He cheered and heckled for Detroit sports teams, waving a bicycle pump ("Let's get pumped up!") or a banana ("Let's go bananas!") or some other corny prop. A retired schoolteacher with nine children, he always wore a tie and white shirt at the ballpark like he was going to work. And in a way he was. When he heckled, said blogger Karen Bush, "you couldn't *not* hear him."

Legendary Detroit heckler Joe "The Brow" Diroff.

deal. No other city can compare to Philly when it comes to cheesesteaks or heckling. To give you a flavor of what it is like there, let's look at the city's major sports teams, beginning with the club that has heard the heckling and the boos the longest.

The Phillies

Since the 1880s the Phillies have been Philadelphia's major league baseball representative. (The Athletics also played there for a spell.) The fans there love their Phillies and make it tough on visiting players who challenge them, as these major leaguers have testified over the years:

> Matt Kemp: "Philadelphia fans, by far. They're the toughest. They say whatever is on their mind at any given moment. They don't care."

> C. C. Sabathia: "They have tough fans. They're all over you constantly."

> Brian McCann: "Philly gets on me. Every time I go in there, I'm getting heckled. They call me everything. They get on me pretty hard."

> Carl Crawford: "The toughest city I've ever played in has to be Philadelphia. Fans are tough there. We played them there in the World Series and I've never seen nothin' like it."

Crawford was referring to the 2008 World Series, between Tampa Bay and Philadelphia, and what he and other Rays experienced in Philly is still seared into their memories like the death of a loved one. "Whatever the opposite of hospitable would be," said Crawford's teammate Rocco Baldelli, "that's what the people of Philadelphia were to us at that time." The Rays took the team bus to Citizens Bank Park before Game 3, their first appearance in town. Fans there lined the street and flipped them off and banged the bus with their fists. "The fans lived up to their belligerent level," said pitching coach Jim Hickey. "They wear it as a badge of honor."

Hickey said that his ex-wife had to call security because she and other Tampa Bay supporters were being harassed in their seats by Phillies fans. But security, he said, did nothing—a classic example of how a rule about fan behavior may be on the books but subject to how ushers and security enforce it, if they enforce it at all. "There was a kid by the bullpen cursing at us and there was a cop there just laughing at us," said bullpen catcher and coach Scott Cursi.

Philadelphia won the series in five games, so millions of Phillies fans probably joined in the laughter. If you're looking for tea and sympathy, you have come to the wrong place. Philly fans are tough on everybody, including their own.

It was Bobblehead Day at Citizens Bank Park for Mike Lieberthal, a man who had spent 13 seasons as a catcher for the Phillies. Nonetheless, one disgruntled fan, unhappy with his performance that day, cried out, "Hey Lieberthal, you suck and your bobblehead is ugly."

One of the greatest Phillies ever was third baseman Mike Schmidt, who, disgusted by fan behavior at Veterans Stadium (the prior home of the team), compared it to an "uncontrollable mob scene." The mob—sorry, Phillies fans—did not appreciate this and Schmidt went from hero to ungrateful punk overnight. Knowing he had picked a fight with the wrong people, a fight he was not going to win, the future Hall of Famer ran out onto the field for the next game wearing a wig and fake glasses, as if to hide his identity. Fans liked the joke and appreciated his show of contrition but still booed him.

"I think there's a little boo in all of us," said Bob Dylan, and if that's true then there's a little of Philadelphia in all of us, because nobody boos more than Philly fans. "They have

In Philly, kids heckle their bobbleheads.

Easter egg hunts in Philadelphia and if the kids don't find the eggs, they get booed," said Bob Uecker in a classic line that has been echoed many times over the years. Pat Burrell starred on that Phillies team that beat Tampa Bay. But the next year he signed a huge deal with those very same Rays and left town. Fans never forgot—and never forgave. When he finally returned to Philadelphia after joining the San Francisco Giants, Phillies fans blistered him with boos and taunts and signs that said, WE'RE SORRY, HIPPIE, WIFE CHEATER, and FAT SLOB.

Phillies fans can claim one of the cleverest bits of heckling done anywhere in recent years. All-Star reliever Craig Kimbrel has one of the most unusual pitching motions in the game, leaning his body forward on the mound and sticking his left arm out like the wing of some weird prehistoric bird. Fans behind home plate at Citizens Bank Park seized on this peculiarity one night and, in an impromptu piece of crowd mockery, stood up and spread their arms like birds at the same time Kimbrel was doing it on the mound. They would stand in this position until he began his motion to throw, at which point they'd sit down. Kids did it, grown-ups did it, everybody. Some of them squawked like birds too. "They're up, ready," said the TV announcer who caught on to what the fans were doing and brought it into his play-by-play. "That's outstanding." And it was.

The Eagles

The Philadelphia Eagles now play at Lincoln Financial Field. But like the Phillies, for many years their home was Veterans Stadium, which contained a holding cell for the rowdiest fans who were deemed to be a public safety threat. The cell—probably more of a drunk tank—kept the fans on ice until a judge at the stadium could hold hearings to determine what punishment, if any, they would receive. Citing this and other examples of their churlish behavior—such as the time they cheered when Dallas Cowboys receiver Michael Irvin was carted off the field on a stretcher with a career-ending neck injury—*Sports Illustrated* dubbed Eagles fans "the most hated" in the NFL.

The most famous incident in Philly fan history—probably the most famous fan incident ever—took place on December 15, 1968, when a big storm dropped a foot of snow on the city.

When fans arrived at Franklin Field, where the Eagles were playing, they had to push snow off their seats. Although the skies cleared by game time, it was still blisteringly cold. Few of the faithful were in a good mood. Spoiling their mood still more was the woeful state of the Eagles, who sucked as a team but unfortunately did not suck quite enough, losing out on the right to pick No. 1 in the upcoming NFL draft. If they had remained winless, as they had been earlier in the year, they could have chosen college football's best player, USC running back and future Hall of Famer O. J. Simpson. But they blew

Comic goes off on Philly, Philly loves it

All things considered, comedian Bill Burr, like many pro athletes, would rather not be in Philadelphia. A few years ago he played a comedy club in nearby Camden but his act did not go well, the audience heckling and jeering and booing him after every failed joke. This pissed him off, causing him to unleash an epic, expletive-laced diatribe against Philadelphia and its sports teams that YouTubers have watched more than a million times. Some (cleaned-up) excerpts:

"F**king Rocky is your hero. The whole pride of your city is built around a guy who doesn't even exist."

"You know what, you losers? I hope the Eagles never win the Super Bowl. All of you in your Donovan McNabb shirts. I hope he snaps both his ankles the first time they have a game. You guys haven't won a Super Bowl since they had face masks."

"The Flyers—do they even exist anymore? A buncha damn pansies. They haven't won sh*t since Gerald Ford was in office. They should have the Ice Capades down there now. You probably wouldn't even know the difference."

"What's left? The Phillies. Named after a female horse. You bunch of p*ssies. One World Series since the 1880s? Bring Tug McGraw back from the dead, maybe you'll win another one. But it ain't ever happening with that candy-striped uniform. They should be selling cotton candy in the instructional leagues."

Surprisingly, or perhaps not so considering the toughness of Philly audiences, Burr's rant won him laughs. And a grudging respect. People seemed to appreciate his real anger, his real intensity. After finishing up with one last Rocky joke—"You all gonna go see *Rocky 19*? Hey dude, I think he can win!"—he left the stage as the emcee walked on and said, "You guys, let's hear it for Bill Burr!" The audience cheered; nobody booed.

their chance by winning three games, giving them a lower pick and sinking them permanently into a dismal mediocrity.

Seeking to brighten things up and create some holiday cheer, Eagles management staged a Christmas halftime show with high-kicking cheerleaders and a peppy marching band. But the star of the show got stuck in Atlantic City due to the bad weather, forcing organizers to hastily recruit a 19-year-old Philadelphian, Frank Olivo, to step in and play Santa Claus. Olivo was the right man for the job because it was his personal tradition to come to the final home game of every Eagles season dressed as Santa, complete with beard and red suit. Since he already looked the part, all he had to do was walk down the center of the field and wave to fans and act cheery.

Cue the band. As it played the Gene Autry favorite "Here Comes Santa Claus," the agreeable Olivo did as he was told—walking from one end zone to the other and then back along the running track that encircled the football field. The fans responded by doing what felt right to them: They booed. They booed Santa Claus. "They booed loudly the moment he hit the field, and when he made it to the track, he was in range. The snowballs started flying, hitting him in his jolly front and back," wrote reporter Casey Matthews in an ESPN retrospective decades later. Olivo's cousin described it as "a tsunami of snowballs" raining down on him, hitting him in the face and body and knocking off his fake white eyebrows, until finally he escaped out of harm's way.

Decades later, his place in Philadelphia sports history secure, Olivo was anything but bitter about the incident. Just the opposite. He remained a die-hard Eagles fan and proudly supportive of the city whose fans once pelted him with

Santa being welcomed by
Philadelphia fans.

snowballs. "Philadelphia sports fans have the reputation for being the worst in the country, and it's bull," he told Matthews. "Because the Philadelphia sports fan, regardless of whether the team is good or bad, they will fill these stadiums, they'll put their money out to go to these games, they'll support the team. They're smart fans. They live and die with their teams." Olivo was right there with them until his death in April 2015.

The 76ers

Another date in Philly fan history, not quite as historic as booing Santa but still memorable: February 10, 2002. This was the night of the NBA All-Star Game at First Union Center, home of the 76ers, and the homecoming of Kobe Bryant, a native Philadelphian and area prep star who had gone away to find fame, fortune, and NBA titles with the Los Angeles Lakers. While leading the West to victory he scored 31 points and earned MVP honors. In a special presentation at midcourt after the game, then-NBA Commissioner David Stern called him "the star of stars" and presented him with a trophy that he raised above his head in triumph as Philly fans showered him with cheers and applause.

Uh, well, no, not exactly. Not even close, actually. Philadelphia fans booed him, and the boos were so loud and persistent that Ahmad Rashad, stepping in to interview Kobe after Stern departed, could not ignore them. He asked Bryant what he thought about it. "I know the fans are booing," he said, "but nonetheless it feels good to come home. It's good to play in front of the home crowd."

The smiling Bryant was doing his best to put a positive spin on the situation, as was Rashad. They neglected to mention, however, the events leading up to this moment— how Kobe and the Lakers had met the 76ers in the NBA Finals the previous year, how he had vowed to come back to Philadelphia and "cut their hearts out," and how, most painfully of all, he had done just that, the Lakers winning in five. As the boos kept coming Rashad asked Kobe again for his reaction and the MVP, manfully holding on to that tightly clenched smile, said that "even though the reception isn't that warm, I still enjoy coming back."

Bryant's hostile reception triggered a civic debate in Philadelphia. Many people felt the booing was inappropriate and that he should have received a more gracious welcome. Charles Barkley, a former 76er who had heard more than a few boos in his years in the city, described it as "ugly, mean, and totally unwarranted." The mayor agreed, as did the *Philadelphia Inquirer*, which blasted the fans in an editorial entitled "Bad Attitude." But, as they did with Mike Schmidt, Philly fans struck back at the criticism, raining e-mails like snowballs down on the paper. A few excerpts:

> *"In response to your editorial 'Bad Attitude,' apparently you and everyone else have forgotten that it was Kobe who came 'home' last year for the playoffs . . . and his response was 'his HOME is in L.A., he is an L.A. boy now.'"* —Barbara R. Marchesani, Philadelphia

> *"The self-professed 'L.A. Guy' was the best player in the All-Star game, but he was also a guy in a Lakers uniform at the First Union Center. So, it wouldn't have mattered if he was from Mars."* —Reggie Brashy Jr., Philadelphia

"I don't see why people are making such a big deal over booing Kobe Bryant. . . . Sure, he is from the area, but he left it at the first opportunity and how often do you see him back here in the offseason?" —Jack Redfern, Philadelphia

"Since when has Lower Merion [the suburb where Bryant played high school ball] been considered Philly?" —Cheryl A. Smith, Philadelphia

"I commend my fellow Philadelphians on giving Kobe Bryant the welcome he so deserved. . . . We took him in when his fame took off and how does he repay us for the gratitude we'd given him before? He says he's gonna cut our hearts out and that he's always been an L.A. guy and never a Philly fan." —Kelvin Randell, Philadelphia

And finally, Katy Rawdon-Faucett of the Philadelphia metro area: "As to why Bryant is so disliked here—that's easy. . . . Kobe Bryant comes off as a smug, arrogant jerk. . . . If there's one thing Philadelphia fans can't stand, it's disloyalty. Just ask Eric Lindros."

Glad you brought him up, Katy. Since he's a hockey guy, let's consider him in the next chapter. Philly gave him a pretty good thrashing too.

CHAPTER 13

The curious case of the hockey heckler

In 2002, when that Philly fan mad at Kobe Bryant also took a shot at Eric Lindros in a letter to the *Inquirer*, memories of his time in the city were still sharp and filled with pain and disappointment. One of hockey's biggest names, arguably the best power forward of his era, Lindros played eight mostly successful seasons with the Philadelphia Flyers before being traded to the New York Rangers. Despite his success he and his teammates had never been able to deliver what Philly fans wanted most: a Stanley Cup. He had left town amidst accusations that he had quit on the team and was only looking out for himself and money, like so many other ungrateful professional athletes, the story goes.

In January, only a month before the Kobe Bryant All-Star game, Lindros made a Philadelphia homecoming of his own, returning to the city for the first time since becoming a New York Ranger. And how did Philly fans welcome him back?

Well, you know the answer to that. "No place on earth was flushed with more sporting emotion Saturday than a parcel of land near the corner of Broad and Pattison," writes reporter Jeff Jacobs. "At the First Union Center [now Wells Fargo Center], 19,867 Flyers fans came to thank Lindros for a decade of brilliance in the only way they knew how. They booed his name. They booed his jersey. They booed him every time he touched the puck."

They booed him when he skated onto the ice for warm-ups, and they booed him when he skated off the ice at game's end. During time-outs the Flyers held a trivia contest for fans and showed pictures of them on the screen. One woman was asked what Flyer player had won an Olympic medal. When she answered, "Eric Lindros," the fans booed her. Quickly realizing her mistake, she apologized for mentioning the outcast's name.

The last time Lindros suited up for the Flyers was in Philadelphia for Game 7 of the 2000 Eastern Conference finals against the New Jersey Devils. The Flyers lost both Lindros and possibly the game on the same play, when Devils defenseman Scott Stevens laid a hit on him that blogger John Fischer described as "fantastically brutal." New Jersey was leading 1–0 in the first period and Lindros was coming across the ice with the puck, getting ready to shoot and looking away when Stevens came up on him, lowered his left shoulder, and made hard contact. NFL linebackers have not delivered hits with as much force. It struck Lindros in the jaw, snapped his head back, and dropped him to the ice like a heavyweight boxer falling to the canvas after a punch. When he fell his helmet stayed on but his head bounced against the ice, hard.

It was a clean and legal body check that brought the game temporarily to a halt as the dazed Lindros lay on the ice. Eventually he was helped to his feet by two teammates who slowly skated with him off the ice. He may not have been able to do it on his own power. The normally vocal Philadelphia crowd grew unusually quiet and subdued, murmuring their discontent as Lindros left, not to return. The Flyers players and coaches appeared to share their concern. All seemed to recognize what the hit potentially meant to the game—Philly ultimately lost 2–1 and New Jersey went on to win the Cup—and to Lindros personally.

Afterward he was diagnosed as having suffered a concussion, his sixth as a member of the Flyers. (He would have at least one more serious one before retiring in 2007.) He had a concussion earlier that season and four others the previous two years, beginning in 1998 with another legal but brutal hit by Darius Kasparaitis of the Pittsburgh Penguins. ESPN's David Fleming wrote that Lindros was so out of it after that game that he "didn't recognize his surroundings."

Because of these troubles, if you didn't know hockey you might think Lindros was a tiny little guy whom the big, bad bullies of the NHL kept picking on. Nothing could be further from the truth. The 6-foot-4, 230-pounder was one of the biggest, strongest and most powerful power forwards whose style of play one reporter likened to a wrecking ball. Big No. 88 flattened opponents as clean and hard as Kasparaitis and Stevens had done to him. According to Drop Your Gloves, a website that tracks the pugilistic exploits of ice hockey players, his fight record was 38 wins, 2 losses, 10 draws. Its system determines wins and losses based on the number of punches thrown and landed. Lindros did not lose a fight until his fourth season in the NHL, when Marty McSorley of the Los Angeles Kings got the better of him, throwing 24 punches and landing 15 compared to Lindros's 7 and 4. His only other loss came to Derian Hatcher of the Dallas Stars, but this was a much closer fight, Hatcher landing 12 punches to 7 by Lindros. Apart from these two, though, the Big E threw his weight around pretty good on the ice. If you messed with him, generally you got messed with. Big time.

One of his greatest fights occurred in 1993; his opponent was Scott Stevens of the New Jersey Devils, the man who would knock him out with that ferocious hit seven years later. But this was before all the concussions. Lindros was young, only 20 and in his drop-your-gloves prime, and Stevens was pushing 30. He stood 2 inches taller and was by far the bigger and stronger man. He overwhelmed Stevens and landed punch after punch with no answer. He basically beat the snot out of him.

Stevens, a known and respected enforcer around the league, was testing the mettle of Lindros, who was then in his rookie season with the Flyers and, although barely out of his teens, already a controversial figure in hockey. The controversy stemmed from his refusal to play for the Quebec Nordiques after the Nordiques drafted him first overall in the 1991 NHL Draft. The Nordiques, based in Quebec City in the French Canadian province of Quebec, regarded Lindros as a potential franchise player, a big, fast, super-skilled talent who could lead them to the Stanley Cup, the Wayne Gretzky of his generation. One hitch though: This Great One wasn't going to play there. Unhappy with the team's ownership, its sad-sack record, and

Throwing things on the ice

The National Hockey League's official Fan Code of Conduct prohibits "disruptive or inconsiderate behaviors or unruly actions" by fans. Fans can neither "interfere with the event and/or athletes in any manner" nor use "abusive language or obscene gestures." In what may come as a shock to many hockey fans, they also cannot throw things on the ice.

Here is the exact wording: "Fans may not engage in fighting, throwing objects or other behavior deemed detrimental to the experience" of other fans at the game. This may be shocking news because throwing crap on the ice is one of hockey's oldest and grandest traditions. Here are a few of the things fans have thrown over the years, happily and unhappily:

Beer (cups, bottles, cans), beef, chairs, coins of all kinds, dildos, eggs, fish, chickens (frozen and rubber), firecrackers, fruit (lots of tomatoes), hats and hats and hats, iron bolts, leopard sharks, lightbulbs, octopi (hello, Detroit!), pucks, pacifiers (see Lindros, Eric, in Quebec City), rubber rats, squid, trash, waffles, and women's panties.

Throwing crap on the ice—a grand old hockey tradition.

As to whether you should follow the NHL's code of conduct and refrain from throwing things on the ice, we will leave that up to you and your conscience.

the city and people—the gifted but petulant teenager made remarks dissing French-Canadians and Quebecois culture— he refused to report to Quebec. Ever. A long and contentious standoff ended with the Nordiques sending him to Philadelphia in what is considered one of the biggest trades in NHL history.

After becoming a Flyer, Lindros's first game in Quebec City after the trade was similar to his first appearance in Philadelphia some 10 years later as a New York Ranger, only worse. Asked beforehand what he thought his reception would be like, he said, "I don't expect roses. I don't expect any gifts. Just regular boos. That should do it. It's just a hockey game." He did not get roses. Nor were the boos of the regular sort; they were loud, long, and deeply felt, proving, if proof was needed, that booing and heckling are hardly American phenomena. They know how to do it quite well in French-speaking Quebec too.

A Quebec radio station handed out pacifiers to fans as they entered the arena, and the fans threw them at Lindros and onto the ice. Periodically play was stopped to clear them away. The action would resume only to be stopped a while later as more pacifiers bombarded the ice. This happened repeatedly but the PA announcer never warned the fans about throwing things on the ice, never told them to stop. What makes this even more noteworthy was that then-NHL president Gil Stein occupied a seat in the arena near the Nordiques' bench, and one of the pacifiers hit him. Clearly, the unhappy Nordique fans were going to have their say, and no league or team or arena official was going to say boo about it.

Some hairy-chested fans shed their shirts and dressed up like babies. They wore diapers over their pants and baby

Let them know they're babies.

bonnets and waved rattles and oversize pacifiers. One sign showed a picture of a giant pacifier with the message: *Bebe Lindros. Bon Debarras*! Good riddance, you baby.

The theme of the night centered on Lindros's youth, his immaturity, his tantrum-like refusal to play for the Nordiques, and the fact that he was not that far removed from the under-20 Canadian junior hockey leagues, where he had starred for the champion Oshawa Generals. Oshawa is in the province of Ontario, whose capital city is Toronto. Lindros grew up in western Ontario, but his family moved to Toronto when he was a boy so he could go to school there and play junior hockey. Canadian hockey devotees followed Lindros and tagged him for greatness as early as grade school.

Ice hockey is Canada's national sport, and hundreds of thousands of children, both boys and girls, play on junior teams across the country beginning at age four. One such Junior B team is St. John's Caps, located in the city of St. John's on the island of Newfoundland on Canada's remote and ruggedly beautiful northeastern coast. Now, ordinarily what goes on in youth hockey in St. John's is not a matter of much concern to Americans or even most Canadians. But that was before a self-professed "hockey heckler" named Corey Simms entered the scene and started stirring things up.

With thinning hair and a goatee, Simms is a die-hard St. John's Caps fan and a frequent sight at their home games, dressed in his hooded black Caps sweatshirt with red lettering. It is not the sight of him that disturbs so many, but his constant badgering and hectoring of St. John's opponents. "He's screaming and yelling at the players," says Kevin Tobin, an executive with the Conception Bay Junior Renegades, a rival team. "It's different than heckling like, 'Come on, come on, you can do better than that,' or trying to poke fun at certain players. . . . It's just constant, constant, constant."

The players targeted by Simms range in age from 18 to 22—old enough, in his view, to take what he is dishing out.

Tobin does not think so. Nor did the St. John's Junior Hockey League president, who sent him a letter ordering him to stay away from the season-ending playoffs and indicating that he would not be permitted to enter any ice rinks where the games were being held. Several arenas had already banned him. When Simms said no, not gonna do that, if the Caps were playing he was going to be there, Tobin's Renegades bowed out of the playoffs and forfeited their semifinal game against St. John's rather than subject themselves to his heckling. The league evidently cannot enforce a ban against him at ice arenas open to the public.

All this hockey fighting off the ice caught the attention of the local media, and a Newfoundland TV station sent a camera crew over to Twin Rinks ice arena to talk to Simms to see what he had to say.

This was when things got really interesting.

Katie Breen, the reporter covering the story, introduced Simms to her viewers this way: "To Corey Simms, heckling is a part of the game, just like fist fighting and losing teeth. He knows his antics get under everyone's skin, but he says, 'Suck it up.'"

And then Breen put Simms on camera and asked him what he thought of his critics. And he said, basically, just that: Suck it up, people.

"If the hockey moms can't handle me yelling and heckling at the rinks, I think they should stick to crosswords and knitting," he said. "And if the young boys—young men, I should say—can't handle a bit of heckling at the rink, they should stick to tiddlywinks and PlayStation."

Breen agreed with him on one point, that the older teen players in the league were "not kids." But she quoted one of his critics—one of those hockey moms—who claimed that he had once yelled that he was "going to rip [a player's] head off and clean the ice with it."

"Come on," said Simms when he heard this. "I mean, come on, that's disgusting. Besides that, I'm not a terrorist. That's ISIS stuff. Come on." He concluded his self-defense by saying, "I'm just a heckler. I'm that guy, a local legend for hecklers. I heckle all hockey games. It's who I am. I'm a heckler."

Once Breen's report appeared on the world's video bulletin board, YouTube, it circulated around the United States and Canada and showed, once again, that some of the most vicious hecklers you will ever find are in the media. One might even say that a heckler is a critic without credentials. In any event reporters, bloggers, and radio sports talk show hosts universally trolled him for being, as Vice Sports termed it, "the world's biggest loser." The *Toronto Sun* described him as "an agitator" and "a well-known junior hockey heckler who wants people to know two things: He's not a terrorist. And he's not part of ISIS." To CBC News he was "abusive." The *Los Angeles Times* said Simms "may not try to rip your head off and clean the ice with it . . . But he just might get you with a zinger involving knitting and tiddlywinks."

"Do you remember when you found your calling?" wrote Deadspin. "It might have happened at a different point in your life than your parents, siblings, or friends. Corey Simms found his about five years ago while watching the St. John's Caps . . . He decided to yell at their opponents." "And now we give you a guy who has taken heckling to horrifying (and hilarious) levels," said Yahoo! Sports. "Corey Simms, explain to us why you love the St. John's Caps and why you heckle the crap out of their opponents." "This guy can't be real life," agreed Barstool Sports. "Is this a Kimmel prank? It has to be, right? What an unbelievable character. I could be a heinous terrorist that beheads people for a living but instead I decided to be a hockey heckler."

In a sport whose core values include toughness and fighting, Simms had hit below the belt. Or so said his critics, who failed to note that if he had done his heckling at an NHL game, he would have caused nary a ripple, being one small voice among many. But since he was doing it at junior games in tiny, out-of-the-way rinks, everything he said could be *heard*. His lone voice stood out, not drowned out by the crowd because there wasn't much crowd to speak of.

Save for a few interested locals, the only people who consistently attend junior games—who care about them enough to go—are the parents of the players. Also family members and close friends, yes. But mainly parents. Hockey moms and hockey dads were sick of Simms verbally abusing their children, and they wanted it—needed it—to stop. *Now!* And they may have been absolutely right.

But this curious, compelling case reveals a truth about youth sports in general. If you talk to people actively involved in youth sports—parents, coaches, managers, referees, umpires, league officials, players—virtually everyone agrees on who the biggest troublemakers are. Who yells the most. Who is the most irrational, emotional, even violent. Who is the most intrusive. Who endlessly kvetches about referees, coaches, players. Who is, in short, the biggest collective pain in the a**.

Parents, that's who.

What should we do as a society about this constantly irritating, disruptive, abusive group of hecklers? Well, that is a subject for another time. As for Eric Lindros, after retiring from the game he and Philadelphia fans patched up their differences, and in 2015 he was inducted into the Philadelphia Flyers Hall of Fame. Some think his sterling 13-year NHL career—including multiple All-Star selections, a Hart Memorial Trophy, and many other awards—merits him entry into the Hockey Hall of Fame. When he retired he donated $5 million to the Ontario acute care medical center that treated him for the concussions that

The irrational, emotional, and violent hockey mom.

marred his career. He met and married a woman from Quebec City—the once-hostile home of the Nordiques, who long ago left town and relocated to Denver—and he happily reports no lingering effects from those concussions. He is in robust good health.

CHAPTER 14

The royal and ancient heckling game

Then there was golf. Thankfully amidst the messiness of modern sports and life, the rise in cursing and incivility, the decline of standards, the collapse of public morals, the attack, at bottom, against Western Civilization and all the values we hold dear, the blessed ancient Scottish links game has held the line, stemmed the tide, blunted the outrages, and maintained a level of fan decency, decorum, and polite behavior that is an inspiration for other sports and a model to which they can dream and aspire.

"Bullsh*t!" as a heckler might say.

The barbarians have stormed the gates of golf as well. Hecklers are showing up in country clubs and at major golf tournaments, producing incidents such as these.

"Cheater"

At the 2015 U.S. Open in Chambers Bay, Washington, a plane pulling a "Cheater" banner circled in the air above Tiger Woods on the course, causing gossips to wonder if this was yet another slap at Tiger's divot-filled love life, specifically his breakup with American World Cup skier Lindsey Vonn, who had just dumped him, apparently because of his less-than-faithful adherence to a monogamous boyfriend-girlfriend relationship. Another heckler

Aeronautically heckling Tiger Woods.

at Chambers Bay, also taking sides in the spat, shouted "Lindsey Vonn" at him. "You can block it out as many times as you can," Tiger has said about heckling, "but after a while you're going to snap." Fortunately Tiger did not snap at these provocations and soldiered on.

Screaming on the backswing

It was Sunday, the final round of the 2015 Memorial at Muirfield Village in Ohio, and Justin Rose had just made birdie to put him in the lead by a stroke. On the 14th hole his drive landed in a greenside bunker with the flag in front of him. Looking at an easy chip-in for par, he drew his wedge back, and as his club started to come forward a fan screamed, shattering his concentration and causing him to chunk his shot. The ball went awry, and Rose looked over in hopeless frustration at the man who yelled.

Don't yell during a golfer's backswing? *Ahem.*

That easy par turned into a bogey, dropping him back into a tie with four holes to go. He finished regulation in a tie but lost the tournament in a playoff. Many observers blamed the loss on the heckler, who apparently had acted deliberately to sabotage Rose, who is English. "Some people think yelling at golf tournaments is fun and should be encouraged," wrote blogger Luke Kerr-Dineen. "Others consider it detestable and think perpetrators should be banned. But everyone agrees that no one should yell in the middle of a golfer's backswing."

Rose, a U.S. Open champion, thought the heckler's action was part of a larger issue having to do with golf's popularity and the public's changing view of golfers themselves. "It is a professional sport and in other sports players are encouraged to play through the noise," he said. "But I think we are being forced to become entertainers. The ropes have been brought in close because every sponsor is trying to give the fans more access to us."

"Fried chicken!"

Few golfers have had more experience with "the increasingly rowdy PGA Tour," as it has been described, than Sergio Garcia. One could also argue that few golfers have done more to irritate fans than Garcia, who is known for his at times peevish behavior on the course. His remark about Tiger Woods—whose mother is Asian, his father black—and how he, Sergio, could entice Tiger to come to dinner by serving him fried chicken, repeated the old racial stereotype that African Americans love fried chicken above all. Garcia later apologized.

Not long after making the remark the Spaniard appeared at a U.S. Open near Philadelphia and needed extra security to protect him from inhospitable fans, one of whom shouted "Fried chicken!" just as Garcia was about to tee off. Asked if he would like the heckler removed, Garcia said no, thinking that would only turn the galleries even more against him.

Garcia, a leading golfer on the European tour who has had less success in the United States, has lots of American followers who cheer for him. He also has lots who don't. At a Players Championship he stroked a putt on the 17th hole at TPC Sawgrass in Florida, the picturesque island green almost completely encircled by water. As the ball started to roll, a fan yelled, "Go in the water!" The ball did not go in the water, nor did it go in the hole, and Garcia finished the end of 72 holes tied for the lead, only to lose his bid for the title in a playoff. As with Justin Rose, some observers felt the heckling that Sergio got—"about three or four times on every hole," he said, on the back nine on closing day—cost him the tournament.

PGA Tour executive Ty Votaw said the heckling was out of keeping with the rules and traditions of golf. "It is our goal to create the absolute best tournament in golf," he told a reporter. "Fans who act inappropriately and affect the tournament experience with disrespectful behavior will be ejected immediately."

"Nice putting, Sally!

Another foreign golfer who has endured the disapproval of domestic audiences is Ian Poulter, an Englishman who dresses like a dandy and has spiky hair and a spiky wit to match. He is also partial to pants and shirts done up in the Union Jack, the British flag. He encountered hecklers at the same Players Tournament that Garcia did and at the same island green hole, when he was standing over a putt. Fans were shouting at him, and he stepped back and said to them, "Really?" After the putt went in, as he was walking off the green, he said again to the fans, "Really?" and pointed his club at the man who was leading the yelling.

The 17th hole at a TPC tournament is frequently rowdier than any other place on the course; one year at the U.S. Open at Bethpage, New York, a British commentator said the crowds at that hole "often resembled the notorious right field sections at Yankee Stadium." Wherever the rowdiness surfaces, Nick Faldo, the Masters and U.S. Open champion who is now a broadcaster, urged Poulter to ignore it. "It's the 90 percent–10 percent rule," he said. "Hopefully you please 90 percent because the other 10 percent, you got no chance."

Clearly that 10 percent has it in for Poulter. After he missed a putt at the Chambers Bay U.S. Open, someone in the gallery said, "Nice putting, Sally." The Brit cupped his ear to show he had heard the remark and did not like it.

"Shhhhhh"

Plenty of heckling goes on overseas and is done by Europeans. If there are Ugly Americans in golf there are Ugly Brits, Ugly Scots, Ugly Spaniards, and Ugly Europeans too. American Patrick Reed can testify to this after missing a short putt on the 16th hole at Gleneagles in Scotland during a Saturday afternoon Ryder Cup match. Fans of the European side—the Ryder Cup pits the United States against Europe in team play—roared their approval. Then, the next day, before he was about to take his tee shot on the first hole, a British fan needled him by asking him if he had practiced his putting last night.

The heckling and pro-European cheers continued unabated until the seventh hole, where Reed silenced the crowd by sinking a tough birdie putt to pull himself into a tie with the European he was facing. The fired-up Reed mocked the fans by putting his index finger over his lips and shushing them, then thrusting his arms upward to pump up the American supporters in the gallery.

"No Love!"

"Unlike other professional sports where loud noise is commonplace," writes Stephen Hennessey of *Golf Digest*, "our game is associated with an etiquette and tradition. Yet there still appears to be a divide amongst golf fans whether heckling and random bursts of yelling should be tolerated or not."

Put Davis Love III down as a vote for no tolerance. At a Match Play Championship in Carlsbad, a heckler shouted "Whoop!" after he missed a par putt and followed it up by yelling "No love!" as the golfer stepped up to hit driver on the next hole. Love refused to play anymore until officials silenced the man. Ultimately they escorted him off the grounds. A similar thing happened to a heckler at Bay Hill when he taunted Love for poor Ryder Cup play.

Asked why bad fan behavior in golf seems on the upswing, Love, the 2016 U.S. Ryder Cup team captain, thinks some of it has to do with society at large: "I think it's our whole society. They don't respect what other people do, don't respect your elders, don't respect other people's space, don't respect traditions or etiquette or customs. You see it in every sport."

Things to yell after a tee shot

Andrew Widmar was a Pepperdine University student who found a creative way to send a message to his mother back home in Texas. Pepperdine is in Malibu, and a few years ago Tiger Woods was playing in a PGA tournament nearby. Andrew told his mom that he was going to the tournament, which was being televised, and that she should watch Tiger play the 18th hole on Sunday because he and his buddies were going to yell "Mashed potatoes!" after Tiger's drive. It was his way of saying hi to her.

They did—and posted the video on YouTube, which helped start the trend of guys yelling "Mashed potatoes!" after tee shots. "It's a good one to yell because it's nice and quick and means absolutely nothing," Andrew explained.

Other golf fans yell meaningless things too. Here is a brief rundown of the things they yell and the general categories they fall into.

Food. Besides mashed potatoes, other food-related shouts have been used, such as "Filet mignon!" and "Medium rare!" If there are two of you, one can shout the type of steak he likes and the other can follow with how he likes it cooked. Some have yelled "Mango chutney!" You can always cook up your own phrase. "Chicken salad!" or "Beans and rice!" might work.

Inspirational. Yelling something at a golfer midswing is bad form and will likely get you escorted off the grounds. Yelling something *before* he hits is somewhat tolerated, as long as it is positive and encouraging. These include "Knock it in the tooth!" and "Light the candle!" Shouting "Bunker!" after a player hits is not considered positive and may draw unwelcome attention for you. "Fill my hole!" has unsavory sexual implications. One goofy expression to get a golf ball up and going is "Five-hour energy!"

Pop culture. Some golf fans mimic the old Fred Flintstone cartoon character and yell "Yabba-dabba-doo!" Others channel Sly & the Family Stone and sing out "Boom-sha-ka-laka!" *Star Wars* fans have been known to growl like Chewbacca after the ball takes flight. Pro golfers as well as spectators scratched their heads over "Baba Booey!" It is a Howard Stern reference shouted out by fans of his radio show. If done right, one of the funniest things to yell after a good tee shot is "Yeah playa," done perhaps in an old-school Luther Vandross or Barry White voice.

Old school. For a time on golf courses across America, people would yell, "Let the big dog eat!" after a tee shot. Fortunately the big dog doesn't dine out as much anymore. Variations on the canine theme are "Let the big dog hunt" and "That dog has gotta hunt!" "You the man!" is another old-school postdrive shout. "Get in the hole!" has been around forever and probably always will be because it is such a succinct expression of what we all want the ball to do after we hit it.

Heckling "Mrs. Doubtfire"

If, as Love says, antisocial behavior is on the rise, it may have something to do with technology. In Ben Hogan's or Bobby Jones's time, nobody carried camera phones, there was no Internet, and nobody uploaded videos of fans acting up so that others could watch and share them. People see things that are edgy and funny online and they decide to copy them, on a golf course and tournament near them.

Golf itself may need to accept some responsibility. The Ryder Cup is incredibly exciting and has brought tremendous enthusiasm and passion to the sport. But as the rivalry between the United States and Europe has grown fiercer over the years, so has the rambunctiousness of the galleries. Players for both teams whip up the crowds and the crowds happily get whipped up, cheering and heckling and acting in nontraditional ways—nontraditional for golf, that is. Many fans, and not just younger ones, struggle with this contradiction. So at appropriate moments at a Ryder Cup you can scream like a teen girl at a Justin Bieber concert, but at the Open or the Masters or most every other tourney you must put a sock in it. Huh? What? Cheer here but not there? To quote Ian Poulter, "Really?"

In Ben Hogan's or Bobby Jones's time, nobody carried camera phones.

Colin Montgomerie was once the Sergio Garcia of his day, a fine and talented championship-level player to whom American audiences did not entirely warm. Similar to Garcia and Poulter, this was in large part due to the Ryder Cup and all those excitable nationalistic feelings that get stirred up by it. Montgomerie is an Englishman and an excellent Ryder Cupper who helped beat the Americans. Back in the late '90s, while playing the U.S. Open at Congressional, he encountered three women who playfully made wolf whistles at him. This sort of heckling he could handle, not so much when some guys joined in. One yelled, "Go home!" Another, "Piss off!" To which the golfer angrily shot back, "Why don't you save that for the Ryder Cup?" This only encouraged the hecklers, the noisiest of whom Montgomerie dismissed as "a pillock."

"Pillock" is an English word for idiot, and Montgomerie himself said he was not being very bright when he said this because it contributed to the idea that he was a thin-skinned Limey who could be easily baited. Syndicated radio host Jim Rome jumped on this, encouraging his listeners to go after Montgomerie at a U.S. Open in San Francisco. Go after him, they did. David Duval, an American who was paired with Montgomerie during one of the rounds, was shocked by what came out of the mouths of fans. "It wasn't like it was a lot of people," he said, "but some of them were brutal. It was way out of line."

The 1999 Ryder Cup was held at Brookline, Massachusetts, a few miles from Boston. Fans there showed Montgomerie as much respect as the colonists did King George. "The heckling became nothing less than vitriolic," he wrote in his autobiography. "The hecklers' only aim was to put me off." One guy yelled a phrase that Montgomerie does not identify—it was probably

"You suck!"—as he was at the top of his backswing. The golfer stepped off, and three people quickly surrounded the heckler, who was escorted off the grounds. Still, the baiting and heckling went on. The American Payne Stewart, who was playing against Montgomerie in the dramatic Sunday singles matches, pointed out hecklers so they could be removed as well. Montgomerie's father, who was visiting the United States from Britain, walked with his son around the course and was "sickened" by what he saw and heard. "In Dad's eyes, it was if the very game had been defiled," said Montgomerie. After the United States clinched the Cup, Stewart conceded his match to the Englishman in a widely praised act of sportsmanship.

One of the indignities that fans at Brookline and elsewhere piled on Montgomerie was to call him "Mrs. Doubtfire," a wicked piece of sarcasm coined by David Feherty. Feherty thought the plumpish, dowdy-looking Brit resembled the Robin Williams character in the movie of the same name, and the dart clearly hit the bull's-eye, because Montgomerie still remembers it with animus. Montgomerie and Feherty are, by all accounts, not weekend golf buddies.

Feherty, a former European Ryder Cupper from Northern Ireland who is now a TV golf commentator and author, has a somewhat different view of heckling because he does a bit of it himself. Not that he condones shouting on the backswing or the more egregious examples of golf heckling; he does not. And he of course understands the difference between playing in the Ryder Cup and PGA and what weekend amateurs do. Still, he recognizes that jokes and good humor are as much a part of the etiquette and traditions of golf as swearing, throwing clubs, gambling, and drinking too much at the 19th hole.

One of his bits for the Golf Channel has him sitting at the teeing ground of a par-3 on a course in Northern Ireland and heckling the amateur duffers who have come to play it. After a bald man tees up his ball, Feherty says, "Playing out of hope and desperation." Then after he hits: "That's a great shot with that swing."

Another man hits and asks, "That's short, is it?" Feherty says, "Yes, it is, but it's all right; the bunker stopped it." After another man's drive: "Look at that. That's nearly on the golf course." When a man puts his ball on the tee, Feherty says, "There's the hard part done. Teed up beautifully." Then after he makes his drive, Feherty adds, "That looked fine until you hit it."

Feherty's heckling is not unlike the remarks that are heard, every day, on golf courses, public and private, all across America and around the world. A Louisville, Kentucky, charity tournament hired comedian Mike Nilsson to heckle golfers when they drove up to play the 17th hole. The idea was, if they liked the heckling or if they wanted to make it stop, they would contribute more money to help the charity. "Welcome to Hole 17," said Nilsson to an arriving foursome. "This is the heckle hole. Hopefully you guys have been having a good day so far. We're about to ruin all that for you."

He went on, "A formidable foursome here, guys. You look like the Four Horsemen of the Dumb-A** Apocalypse. It's the Fab Four. John, Paul, George, and Dumb-A**. That guy is so dumb he got fired from the M&M factory for throwing out the Ws. That guy is so ugly when he was born his parents called him 'Sh*t Happens.' If ugliness was a crime you'd get the electric chair. The stick with a pin on it is called a flag, sir. You might want to aim for that. Hopefully you brought a Weed eater in your golf bag. I think you're gonna need it." And so on.

A charity tournament in Mississippi features "Heckler's Hill," a designated area near a tee where players can sit on their golf carts and shout good-natured abuse at their fellow golfers. Another group of hecklers does not play golf but likes making mischief at the expense of those who do. They sneak up close to where someone is about to hit, then blast a super-loud air horn at just the right moment. Merriment ensues—for the hecklers anyhow.

Then there is the fellow who parks his truck on a road parallel to a fairway at his local golf course. As a golfer rears back his club, the fellow sticks his head out of the window of his truck and screams. When this ruins the golfer's swing, he yells, "Yahh, gotcha buddy" and speeds off. He mixes up his routine by tossing in lewd remarks: "You know you're out here playing golf and somebody's at home plowing your old lady right

Beware of the truck-driving golf heckler!

now." Crazy cackles of glee follow every insult, as he screeches off down the road like an outcast from *The Dukes of Hazzard*. Then he posts these videos online. "It's a hobby of mine," he explains.

It takes all kinds, to be sure, and all kinds of hecklers too. Not caring to publicly offend other golfers but still wishing them ill, some golfers practice what they call "whisper heckling." They say, "You stink. You're a bum. Miss it"—or stronger words—to other players as they are putting or striking the ball. The other players cannot hear them because no one speaks above a whisper, and if a member of the group raises his voice too loud, the other whisper hecklers shush him the way Patrick Reed silenced those unruly Scots. With these pages documenting so many instances of people yelling and screaming and cursing, this seems the perfect way to end this book—with a whisper, not a bang. If you try whisper heckling, be sure to drink heavily. That always helps.

ABOUT THE AUTHOR

Kevin Nelson is the award-winning author of twenty books, including *The Golden Game, a* history of California baseball which received glowing reviews from the *Los Angeles Times*, *San Francisco Chronicle*, *Publishers Weekly*, and *Sports Illustrated*. It was one of only three books nationally to be named a finalist for SABR's best baseball book of the year. Nelson lives in the San Francisco Bay Area with his family. He blogs at WineTravelAdventure.com.

ABOUT THE ILLUSTRATOR

Aaron Dana is an illustrator/graphic artist based out of Boston, Massachusetts, specializing in portraiture and the world of sport. Visit his website at www.aaron dana.com.